D1761226

an illustrated introduction to

THE TUDORS

Gareth Russell

AMBERLEY

London Bridge. (Courtesy of Jonathan Reeve JR1062b10prelims 16001650)

To my sisters,
Lynsey, Jenny and Ashleigh

I would like to thank the staff at Amberley for asking me to write this book, and in particular my editors, Nicola Gale and Christian Duck, my parents Ian and Heather, my sister Jenny, who gave valuable feedback on the first draft, Dr James Davis, Dr Steven J. Gunn, Susan Higginbotham and Claire Ridgway.

First published 2014

Amberley Publishing
The Hill, Stroud
Gloucestershire, GL5 4EP

www.amberley-books.com

British Library Cataloguing in Publication Data.
A catalogue record for this book is available from the British Library.

ISBN 978 1 4456 4121 8 (paperback)
ISBN 978 1 4456 4133 1 (ebook)

Typesetting and Origination by Amberley Publishing.
Printed in Great Britain.

CONTENTS

THE TUDORS
IN FIVE MINUTES

This book attempts to offer a short introduction to a remarkable family who have remained the objects of popular fascination ever since the last ruler of the line died quietly in her bed in March 1603. The Tudors are Britain's most famous royal dynasty, with interest in them still dwarfing the equally important Plantagenet and Stuart clans, their immediate predecessors and successors. Some of the Tudor court's magnificent residences, admittedly much altered, remain and draw in thousands of tourists every year. Flowers are sent annually to the Tower of London to mark the mortuary anniversaries of those members of the family who met their ends behind the fortress's imposing walls. Henry VIII and his family have been immortalised in everything from after-dinner mints bearing their portraits to fancy dress ensembles and boxes of sweets with them, as bejewelled cats, adorning the front.

The Tudors came to power in 1485 at the end of a bloody civil war that was later known as the Wars of the Roses. It had been caused in large part by a breakdown in royal authority after the mental collapse of King Henry VI and the rise of rival claimants to his crown, in the form of his cousins, the dukes of York. The Tudors were therefore determined to prevent a repetition of this tragedy and as a result they fiercely distrusted most of their extended family and their own aristocracy. The Tudor era also coincided with the discovery of the New World and the first English settlements in the Americas, as well as the plantation of central and southern Ireland which resulted in horrific scenes of what we would now recognise as ethnic cleansing, as the English settlements in Munster were subjected to mass murder, gang rape, the mutilation of the female victims, many of whom were then stripped naked, beaten and driven off into the mountains to die of exposure. Centuries of bitterness were slowly being born and violence

Opposite: Henry VIII, after the sketch by Hans Holbein. (Courtesy of Jonathan Reeve JR955b53piv 15001600)

was endemic in the Tudor period, both of the side of the numerous rebels and by the government, who authorised increasingly inventive and horrific methods of public execution to encourage obedience. Henry VIII's break with the Roman Catholic Church resulted in over a century of sectarian unrest and his children swung the country from Protestant (Edward VI) to Catholic (Mary I) and back again (Elizabeth I). A generation grew up struggling to reconcile the Catholicism of their parents' generation with the intoxicating new vigour of Protestantism. Many lives were lost as people, who believed totally in Christianity's message, groped towards a solution, with Henry VIII, who married six times, being the greatest symbol of his country's spiritual uncertainty. But amid the violence and turmoil, the country also witnessed an expansion in trade, a growth in its global power and significance, new and luxurious forms of architecture, a renaissance of the arts that witnessed the careers of William Shakespeare, Christopher Marlowe, Ben Jonson, Hans Holbein, Thomas Tallis and Edmund Spenser.

Perhaps unsurprisingly, plays, novels, television shows, movies and operas, as well as numerous biographies, reflect the reading and viewing public's fascination with the Tudors' incredible story. Katharine Hepburn and Elizabeth Taylor unsuccessfully fought to play Elizabeth I and Anne Boleyn, respectively. Actors as diverse as Bette Davis, Charlton Heston, Flora Robson, Jean Simmons, Keith Michell, Glenda Jackson, Quentin Crisp, Ray Winstone, Joely Richardson and Damian Lewis got to have a crack at bringing Tudor monarchs to life on screen, while Henry VIII's tribe of unlucky wives, their stories sparkling gold dust to dramatists, have been played on stage and screen by, among others, Merle Oberon, Elsa Lanchester, Deborah Kerr, Winston Churchill's daughter Sarah Beauchamp, Maria Callas, Vanessa Redgrave, Charlotte Rampling, Helena Bonham-Carter, Emily Blunt, Natalie Portman and the singer Joss Stone. Dramatising the Tudor royals brought Oscar nominations for Robert Shaw, Richard Burton, Geneviève Bujold and Cate Blanchett, twice, and Academy wins for Charles Laughton in *The Private Life of Henry VIII* (1933) and Dame Judi Dench in *Shakespeare in Love* (1998).

No two imagined portraits from this mini-industry in its own right were ever quite the same and controversy raged, taking on a new life as the spread of the Internet gave fans an opportunity to voice their feelings about each new portrayal. In the summer of 2010, London's Globe Theatre staged the world premiere of Howard Brenton's new play *Anne Boleyn*, which saw the eponymous character depicted as a gutsy and likeable religious firebrand, deeply committed to the advancement of Protestantism. It won awards. At the same time, the literary world was heaping praise on Hilary Mantel's novel *Wolf Hall*, which presented the same character as a hard-as-nails harridan with little to no genuine political or religious views, and precious few redeeming qualities. A novel soon appeared claiming that Elizabeth I had secretly been a man in drag, while a biography of Catherine Howard alleged that Henry VIII might have had a hand in poisoning his own son.

Beyond the seductive and often hugely enjoyable imaginings of fiction, the Tudors' legacy continues to matter, and tangibly so. The alliance between throne and altar that was set up when the Church of England was created by Henry VIII's first divorce in 1533 and then settled by the religious legislation passed by his youngest daughter still exists, with the current sovereign automatically holding the title adopted by Elizabeth I in 1559 – Supreme Governor of the Church of England. Admittedly, a more humble and tactful option than the title Henry VIII picked – Supreme Head. English dominance over the Irish parliament was codified under Henry VII, creating a system that was to last until the Act of Union in 1800. The birth of the British Empire, made possible by Elizabeth I's quarrels with Spain, began under the Tudors, eventually resulting in an imperial system that changed the course of world history and today still exists in its transmogrified legacy of the Commonwealth. Historians, both academic and popular, debate how much of this was intentional and how much was positive, and argue over the inner workings of Tudor government. Neither their politics nor personalities provoke much agreement. In 2010, a biography of a Tudor queen described Henry VIII as 'so dominant a ruler and so forceful a man', while one of Henry himself, published the year before, witheringly concluded that the king was 'both morally and intellectually limited and heavily dependent on others ... He was too self-obsessed to have any vision of a greater or better England.'

This book starts and remains at the top, with the royals who, despite centuries of popular novels which seek to make them relatable, almost just-like-us, were in fact separated by elaborate rituals and religious initiations which made their subjects, and them, believe that they were uniquely special. I have tried to balance the competing demands of popular fascination and political importance, as well as the jaw-dropping intricacies of the monarchs' private lives with their governmental agenda. I have also tried to set out a clear narrative to make this book an easy-to-follow introduction for those who are interested either in finding out more about the dynasty but who feel intimidated by, or disinclined to pursue, the vast body of literature currently available on them.

TIMELINE

1485
Defeat and death of Richard III at the Battle of Bosworth, coronation of Henry VII as King of England and Lord of Ireland.

1486
Marriage of Henry VII to Elizabeth of York. Birth of Arthur, Prince of Wales, at Winchester.

1487
Defeat of the rebellion which aimed to put the pretender Lambert Simnel on the throne.

1491
Birth of Henry VIII at Greenwich Palace.

1494
Poynings' Law creates the superiority of the English parliament over Dublin's in Irish affairs.

1497
Defeat of rebellions against Tudor rule in Cornwall.

1501
Marriage of Arthur, Prince of Wales, to Katherine of Aragon.

1502
Death of Arthur, Prince of Wales.

1509
Death of Henry VII, accession of Henry VIII, followed by his marriage to Katherine of Aragon, Dowager Princess of Wales.

1511
Birth and death of Henry Tudor, Duke of Cornwall.

1516
Birth of Mary I at Greenwich Palace.

1521
Execution of Edward Stafford, 3rd Duke of Buckingham, the king's cousin.

1527
The king proposes marriage to Anne Boleyn.

1529
Cardinal Wolsey is dismissed from office as Lord Chancellor.

1532
Possible date for Henry VIII's marriage to Anne Boleyn, Marchioness of Pembroke. Early 1533 has also been suggested.

1533
Break with Rome creates the Church of England. Birth of Elizabeth I at Greenwich Palace.

1535
Executions of Thomas More and Cardinal John Fisher.

1536
Death of Katherine of Aragon. Arrest, trial and execution of Queen Anne Boleyn. Marriage of Henry VIII to Jane Seymour. Defeat of the Pilgrimage of Grace uprising.

1537
Birth of Edward VI; death of Queen Jane Seymour twelve days later.

1538
Excommunication of Henry VIII by Pope Paul III.

1539
Numerous executions of courtiers accused of complicity in the 'White Rose Intrigue' against Henry VIII's rule. Passing of the Six Articles signals a return to more conservative religious policy in England and Wales.

1540
Marriage of Henry VIII to Anne of Cleves; they divorced six months later. Execution of Thomas Cromwell, the king's chief minister. Marriage of Henry VIII to Catherine Howard at Oatlands Palace.

1541
Execution of Margaret de la Pole, Countess of Salisbury, the king's cousin.

1542
Execution of Queen Catherine Howard at the Tower of London. Defeat of the Scottish army at the Battle of Solway Moss. Birth of Mary, Queen of Scots.

1543
Marriage of Henry VIII to Katherine Parr, Dowager Lady Latimer.

1544
Third Succession Act restores Mary and Elizabeth Tudor to the line of succession, after their brother Edward, Prince of Wales.

1545
Sinking of the *Mary Rose* warship.

1547
Death of Henry VIII at Whitehall Palace, accession of Edward VI.

1549
Kett's Rebellion reflects the peasantry's unhappiness at government actions in the countryside.

1553
Death of Edward VI, accession and deposition of Queen Jane (*née* Grey). Coronation of Mary I.

1554
Defeat of Wyatt's rebellion against Mary I. Execution of Lady Jane and Lord Guildford Dudley at the Tower of London. Marriage of Mary I to Prince Philip of Spain. Resubmission of the English Church to papal control.

1555
Executions by burning at the stake under Mary I begin with the burning of John Rogers, a married Protestant clergyman.

1558
Calais falls to the French armies. Death of Mary I at Saint James's Palace, accession of Elizabeth I.

1559
Act of Uniformity and Act of Settlement re-establish an independent Church of England.

1568
Mary, Queen of Scots, flees to England.

1570
Pope Pius V excommunicates Elizabeth I.

1571
The Ridolfi Plot to assassinate Queen Elizabeth is foiled.

1587
Execution of Mary, Queen of Scots, at Fotheringhay Castle.

1588
Defeat of the Spanish Armada.

1594
Beginning of the Irish rebellion of Hugh O'Neill, Earl of Tyrone, against Elizabeth I.

1603
Death of Elizabeth I at Richmond Palace, accession of James VI, King of Scots.

The marriage of Henry V to Catherine de Valois in the parish church of St John, Troyes, 2 June 1420. (Courtesy of Jonathan Reeve JR1729b90fp85c 14001500)

1

CATHERINE AND OWEN: THE BEGINNINGS OF THE DYNASTY

Appropriately enough, the history of the Tudor dynasty began with the misery of a queen: Catherine de Valois, the youngest daughter of King Charles VI of France, was, at twenty-six, a bored and unhappy prisoner of her widowhood when her handsome Welsh servant Owen Tudor tripped during an energetic dance move and fell into her lap. Catherine had been left a widow with a nine-month-old baby when her husband King Henry V, one of the most successful warriors in English history, died on campaign in 1422. Henry had realised the long-held English dream of subjugating France, and his marriage to its sickly king's beautiful daughter had been the crowning touch to the diplomatic manoeuvres designed to make Henry V heir to King Charles VI. Catherine, 'the bride of peace', would provide children who were half-French, half-English, and who could therefore rule over both countries. King Henry and Queen Catherine were young, energetic, attractive and cultured, and one contemporary wrote admiringly of 'the feasts and ceremony and luxury of their court.' To the medieval eye, royal magnificence was not a sign of personal extravagance but a display of strength, wealth and national pride.

A year later, Henry's premature death left Catherine alone as their baby son was proclaimed King Henry VI. Catherine had no real political role, no husband and she was bored, lonely and pining for romance. Her first fling came four years after her husband's death, when rumour suggested she was involved with Lord Edmund Beaufort, a handsome nineteen-year-old famed for his skills on the battlefield and younger brother to the Duke of Somerset. His elder sister Joan had recently married King James I of Scotland, and anxious to prevent any further increase in the family's power, Parliament passed a bill stipulating that if a dowager queen married without the king's consent, her new husband's lands and possessions would be seized by the Crown.

That legislation rather killed the mood for young Edmund, who went on to a successful military career as commander of the English armies in the wars against France, and it was a dejected and closely watched Queen Catherine who met

Owen Tudor when he, quite literally, fell for her. A fellow Welshman, Robin of Anglesey, wrote that Owen was overcome with 'affection on the daughter of the King of the land of wine', a rather wonderful turn of phrase. Another wrote that after their first proper meeting, Catherine encountered him swimming naked near the palace and was so impressed by a man 'adorned with wonderful gifts of body and mind' that she fell madly in love with him.

Ordinarily, the madly part of 'madly in love' is a pleasant everyday hyperbole, but in Catherine and Owen's case they must have been deeply in love, lust or, most probably, both to take the kind of risks they did when they secretly married. Marrying beneath one's status was a fairly common and sometimes even sensible move for royal and aristocratic widows, because it meant the new husband could not exert too much influence over his wife or be accused of marrying her to increase his own family's power; status might even out the imbalance of power created by gender. Both of Henry VIII's sisters, Margaret and Mary, did the same after their respective first husbands, the kings of Scotland and France, predeceased them. Jacquetta, Dowager Duchess of Bedford; Anne Boleyn's sister Mary; Katherine Brandon, Dowager Duchess of Suffolk; Queen Katherine Parr; and Frances Grey, Dowager Marchioness of Dorset were other high-profile examples of well-born widows marrying beneath them in the social pecking order. In many of these cases, genuine affection and a taboo passion seem to have spurred the women on to find far greater happiness than they had with their first husbands; as Mary Boleyn said, 'I might a had a greater man of birth and a higher, but I ensure you I could never a had one that should a loved me so well.' Catherine, the daughter, widow and mother of kings, was taking a greater risk because as the widow of a hero-king she was expected to be above reproach; instead, she was marrying far beneath her. Despite what later generations of the Tudor family liked to claim, in 1427 Owen Tudor was nothing more than a down-on-his-luck squire from Anglesey in north-west Wales, whose father Meredith Tudor (Maredydd ap Tudur, in Welsh) had supported the 1400 uprising against King Henry IV. But nothing to his name also meant nothing to lose under the legislation monitoring queens' remarriages, and after their whirlwind romance and elopement, Queen Catherine was apparently heard screaming in orgasmic joy every time they made love.

When news of her remarriage broke, Owen was temporarily arrested and the queen mother was denounced by moralists and courtiers for her inability to control her frail, feminine lust. One contemporary raged that the Welsh were 'vile and barbarous' and that Catherine had disgraced herself by marrying into rebel stock; a later chronicler criticised her for 'following more her own wanton

Catherine of Valois giving birth to the future Henry VI at Windsor Castle. From the *Beauchamp Pageant*. (Courtesy of Jonathan Reeve JR1730b90fp88 14001500)

appetite than friendly counsel, and regarding more private affection than Princely honour', and she was forced to produce documentation before Parliament proving that Owen had enough noble ancestry to be granted the same legal rights as an Englishman. Even more charitable observers, like those who conceded that Catherine had picked 'a right beautiful person' for her husband, could not resist taking swipes at what they considered to be Owen's lower-class origins, describing his cousins as 'men of goodly stature and personage [appearance], but wholly destitute of bringing up'. Later, when she met her in-laws for the first time, Catherine was apparently stunned to discover that there was such a thing as the Welsh language; she spoke several but after they could not find any in common, Catherine cheerfully announced that the Tudors were 'the goodliest dumb creatures that she ever saw.'

The couple produced three sons together, Edmund, Jasper and Owen, before Catherine tragically died in childbirth at the age of thirty-six. The younger

King Henry VI. (Courtesy of Jonathan Reeve JR1561folio6 14001500)

brother, whose name is sometimes confusingly given as Thomas in other accounts, had a monastic vocation, but the two elder boys were invited to court by their fragile and lonely half-brother King Henry VI, who had ignored his advisers' criticisms of his mother and found a great deal of affection for his half-brothers and even his improbable stepfather. Edmund and Jasper were both made earls, with Edmund given significant holdings in the Tudor family's homeland of Wales when he was created Earl of Richmond. As a further sign of royal favour, Edmund was offered the hand of Lady Margaret Beaufort, the precocious niece of Catherine de Valois' one-time suitor, Lord Edmund Beaufort. Intensely pious, the nine-year-old Margaret claimed to have experienced a dream-vision of Saint Nicholas, who told her that marrying Edmund Tudor was part of God's plan for her. They were married once she turned twelve, the age of consent, and she was pregnant within the year. She was a widow seven months later, when her twenty-five-year-old husband died in captivity at Carmarthen in south-west Wales during

Jasper Tudor and his wife Katherine Woodville, Dowager Duchess of Buckingham, from stained-glass windows in Cardiff Castle. (Courtesy of Terry Breverton)

an outbreak of the plague. Terrified, the pregnant Margaret fled to the protection of her brother-in-law Jasper Tudor, Earl of Pembroke.

By 1456, the year of Edmund Tudor's death at Carmarthen, the Lancastrian monarchy was in freefall. The union of the French and English crowns had dissolved as Henry V's death weakened the English hold and Joan of Arc was able to play her celebrated role in galvanising French national spirit against the invaders. Henry VI, who quite possibly suffered from catatonic schizophrenia, suffered lengthening spells of mental stasis in adulthood, which allowed his cousin Richard, Duke of York, to further his own power at the king's expense. Convinced that the Yorks were trying to usurp her husband and son's prerogatives, Henry's fiery queen, Marguerite of Anjou, supported by her friend the Duke of Somerset and by the Tudors, went out of her way to undermine the Yorkist faction at every available opportunity. If her wrath was understandable, it was not always wise and she made many enemies for herself, pushing them into the duke's camp. Recalling that the House of Lancaster had only come to the throne in 1399 by deposing the autocratic King Richard II, the Duke of York and his supporters were able to mount a challenge against the struggling rule of Henry VI that came to be known later as the Wars of the Roses. Edmund Tudor had gone to Carmarthen to establish royal control over the region, but he had fallen into the hands of the Yorkists, caught the plague and died. Three months later, on 28 January 1457, or as the devout Margaret preferred to describe it, the second feast day of Saint Agnes of Rome, his son was born at Pembroke Castle and christened Henry in honour of the beleaguered Lancastrian monarch.

2

HENRY VII: 'IN MARRIAGE AND PEACEABLE CONCORD'

Henry VII was born in Wales at Pembroke Castle on 28 January 1457; his mother cherished it as 'this day of St Agnes, that I did bring into this world my good and gracious prince, king and only-beloved son'. Despite her two subsequent marriages, Henry was to be Margaret Beaufort's only child and through her frantic attempts to delay the marriage of her eldest granddaughter years later, on the grounds that to be impregnated at the age of twelve would 'injure her and endanger her health', we may surmise why.

He was certainly an adored child, cosseted and nurtured behind the imposing walls of Pembroke, his uncle Jasper's residence, until Jasper was driven into exile in 1461 when the Lancastrians lost the civil war and the Duke of York's son took the throne as Edward IV. With Henry VI, his wife and son all fleeing abroad, the kingdom was not safe for the deposed monarch's half-brother, and Jasper sought refuge at the court of King Louis XI of France, who operated under the maxim that England's difficulty was France's opportunity. Pembroke Castle was given to Sir William Herbert, a favourite of the new king; the young Tudor was placed in Herbert's care and separated from his mother, who was sent to live in the household of her new husband, Sir Henry Stafford. For the next eight years, despite his Lancastrian heritage, Henry Tudor was brought up as a ward of the Herbert family and received the typical aristocratic education of etiquette, theology, music (a lifelong passion), languages, dancing, the martial arts, horse riding and hunting. With his descent from Edward III via his mother, and from the kings of France via his grandmother Catherine, he was not a completely unattractive candidate for the Herberts to raise in their midst. His mother's new brother-in-law was the well-connected Duke of Buckingham and there was a chance that, if they could prove themselves loyal, she would be able to get his late father's earldom of Richmond restored to her son. As Margaret networked, Henry grew up, and for a time he was even considered a potential bridegroom for his guardian's daughter, Maud.

Left: Margaret Beaufort, mother of Henry VII, above the gate at Christ's College, Cambridge, one of the many institutions she helped finance. (Courtesy of Elizabeth Norton)

Right: Richard Neville, Earl of Warwick. 'The Kingmaker'. (Courtesy of David Baldwin)

However, in 1470 fortune's wheel moved again when one of Edward IV's hitherto staunchest allies, the Earl of Warwick, deserted him and crossed the Channel to pledge loyalty to Henry VI's exiled queen, Marguerite of Anjou. Warwick's support proved decisive, and his subsequent invasion saw Edward IV take flight as Henry VI was restored to his throne, earning the immensely powerful Warwick the epithet of 'the Kingmaker'. Young Tudor's guardian was captured and executed by Warwick's men, and the boy was brought to London to be reunited with his uncle Jasper, who formally presented him to his uncle the king. By this stage, Henry Tudor was tall with fair skin and dark hair, thin but athletic from a peripatetic lifestyle that required hours spent outdoors and on horseback. He was clever and deeply devout, much like his mother. Uncle Jasper worked hard to rebuild the lad's fortune, but the Lancastrian restoration, later dubbed the Readeption, proved short-lived. At Easter of the following year, the Earl of Warwick was slain, and at the Battle of Tewkesbury the Lancastrians suffered a devastating defeat in which their army was annihilated and the heir to the throne was left dead on the field. Henry VI was captured, brought back to London and quietly murdered in the Tower, with absolutely no-one believing the government's story that he had died of grief.

Correctly predicting that Edward IV would prove far less merciful than he had been the first time he seized the throne, Jasper Tudor grabbed his nephew and with a few loyal followers made a desperate dash for the Welsh coast. At the village of Tenby, they boarded a boat for the Continent. Terrible storms drove them into the harbours of Brittany, which was then an independent duchy under the rule of François II, who granted the Tudor émigrés his protection and refused Edward IV's numerous attempts to have Henry extradited. By a process of brutal elimination, Henry was the de facto head of what remained of the Lancastrian cause and Edward's intentions for him can hardly have been well-meaning.

LIFE IN EXILE

It was in Brittany, separated from his homeland and dependent on another man's generosity, that Henry Tudor grew into adulthood, forming a generally low opinion of mankind's capacity for loyalty. There were some moments of happiness, namely when he fell in love with a young Breton girl whose name is now lost to us and fathered a bastard child by her; the boy, Roland, was protected and financed by his father for the rest of his life. Back in England, his stepfather died in his bed after wounds he incurred in the Wars of the Roses became infected and his widow shrewdly chose as her next husband a Yorkist, Thomas, Lord Stanley, whose connections at Edward IV's court and loyalty to his family might help in her grand quest to rehabilitate her son.

Then, in 1483, Edward IV suddenly died, his once magnificent figure rendered heavy, bloated and worn out by excess at the banqueting table and in the bedroom. His younger brother Richard, Duke of Gloucester, seized the throne as Richard III, deposing his nephew Edward V and launching an attack on his widowed sister-in-law's family, the Woodvilles, which effectively removed them as a force in English politics. The deposed boy king and his younger brother were seen playing in the Tower of London throughout the summer, but they vanished from the records in September of that year. Centuries of speculation and conspiracy theories have attempted to explain what happened to them, with some of the more ludicrously

Richard III with his queen, Anne Neville. (Courtesy of Yale University Art Gallery, Edwin Austin Abbey collection)

hare-brained trying to pin the blame on Henry Tudor's mother, Margaret. The most obvious conclusion remains that they were murdered either on Richard III's orders or by someone very close to him. As king and the boys' legal guardian, Richard bore the ultimate responsibility for their disinheritance and their disappearance. At best, he left them entirely defenceless in a merciless environment and at worst, and most probably, he colluded in or directly ordered their assassination.

The following two years saw Henry Tudor's rapid ascent towards the throne, thanks mainly to his enemies' weaknesses rather than his own strengths. The deposition and disappearance of Edward V split the ranks of the Yorkist nobility, and fifteen weeks after Richard III's coronation his former ally and Margaret Beaufort's one-time brother-in-law, the Duke of Buckingham, attempted to start a rebellion with the express intention of putting Henry Tudor on the throne in Richard's place. Henry was hardly close to the crown in terms of blood, but he was one of the only male candidates left and his mother's descent from one of King Edward III's legitimised grandchildren gave him an admittedly tenuous claim in his own right. Buoyed up by the possibility of becoming king, Henry set sail, but he turned back off the shores of Plymouth when he realised that King Richard's impressive martial skill had ensured the rebellion's failure and Buckingham's subsequent execution. In public, Richard III was superbly disdainful of his rival, 'an unknown Welshman' as he put it, and he described his supporters as 'a company of traitors, thieves, outlaws and renegades'. Privately, however, he was far less sanguine and he increased the pressure on Brittany to hand Henry over for extradition; as François II's mental health failed, his duplicitous treasurer Pierre Landois struck a deal with the English and Henry only narrowly escaped when some of his family's spies at Richard's court tipped him off, giving him enough time to don a disguise and make for the border with France.

From there, he was joined by dozens of disaffected Yorkists as Richard III lost support at a rate not seen in an English kingship in centuries. His retinue's unswerving loyalty made it easy for Richard to seek psychological and political sanctuary in the company of his favourites, particularly as traumas in his private life – the death of his only son in 1484 and then of his queen, Anne Neville, in 1485 – were compounded by political humiliations, chief among which was having to publicly deny that he had poisoned his wife to pave way for an incestuous marriage to his beautiful niece, Elizabeth. The charge was ludicrous, but it helped show how unpopular the king had become, particularly in London, and how insecure his rule was. In the meantime, Henry had scraped together funds for an invasion, liaising with mercenaries and corresponding in secret with his mother, who had used servants, priests and doctors to intrigue with the Dowager Queen Elizabeth Woodville, mother of the vanished Princes in the Tower, from her ecclesiastically guarded sanctuary in Westminster Abbey. Heartbroken and vengeful, Queen Elizabeth had agreed to bless Henry's invasion if, upon its success, he married her eldest daughter, Elizabeth of York, thus uniting the two warring sides of the royal clan for the first time in generations.

Henry, by then twenty-eight, landed in Wales on 8 August 1485, piously kissing the ground as he waded ashore and reciting from the Psalms in Latin. By the time the Feast of the Assumption took place a week later, the gates of Shrewsbury were opening to his army and within a week of that he had reached the heartlands of England almost completely unopposed. If anything, his numbers had increased. The two forces met at the Battle of Bosworth Field on 22 August 1485 and King Richard fought bravely, even as he suffered multiple agonising injuries which were catalogued after the discovery of his remains in 2013. He was eventually killed and taken away for a discreet and minimalist burial. On 31 October, a euphoric Henry was crowned King of England and Lord of Ireland at Westminster Abbey. Eight days later, Parliament issued writs confirming his right to rule, and it was only on 18 January 1486 that he fulfilled his mother's promise and married Edward V's nineteen-year-old sister, Elizabeth of York. His coronation, the sacred right of anointing the king with his divine mandate, had deliberately pre-dated both Parliament's approval and his marriage to the eldest princess of the York

Elizabetha R

Above: Elizabeth of York, wife of Henry VII and mother of Henry VIII. (Courtesy of Ripon Cathedral)

Left: Elizabeth of York. (Courtesy of Amy Licence)

line. Henry wanted to make it crystal clear that the latter only augmented his God-given right to rule. He owed his throne neither to his wife nor his parliament, but solely, like every king since time immemorial, to the Will of Almighty God.

EARLY REIGN

Elizabeth of York, a beautiful young blonde who had inherited much of her parents' good looks but little of their fire, gave birth to her first child nine months after the wedding. It was a boy, christened Arthur in homage to the legends of Camelot and their implicit promise of a reborn British greatness. Only once she had produced an heir was Elizabeth given her own coronation as queen consort, breaking with the medieval tradition which encouraged a bride's coronation shortly after either her marriage or her husband's accession. The ceremony, which harnessed imagery associated with veneration of the Virgin Mary to cast the queen in the light of a mediatory at the heart of government who would intercede for the people and the causes of mercy against the stern justice of the king, mirroring how Mary, Mother of Mercy, would ask the stern but fair God to show clemency to His sinful earthly flock, elevated the queen above all other women in the kingdom. And most of the men. But as one recent history of queenship in England has noted,

> By delaying Elizabeth's ceremony until a year after Arthur's arrival, Henry undid nearly 500 years' worth of accumulated customary power. With the exception of Marguerite of France, whose husband already had an heir, and Anne Neville, whose queenship had not been foreseen, Elizabeth was the only English queen since 1066 to give birth to the king's child without first being crowned. It was marriage to him, he emphasised, that legitimated his heir, and that alone.

The country's relief that uncertainty over the succession had been resolved at the same time as sustained good weather ensured a bumper harvest nurtured popular support for the new king, and a royal tour of the eastern and northern parts of the kingdom, traditionally the most vociferous in their loyalty to the House of York, confirmed the people's good mood. An impressive show of monarchical pomp dazzled the spectators, culminating with Henry's triumphant entry into the city of York itself, which greeted him with pageantry celebrating his marriage to 'their' princess. Heraldic crests of the united white and red roses of the Yorks and Lancasters, later indelibly associated with the entire Tudor family, were complemented by fountains spraying, subtlety of subtleties, rose-water.

men tuum quoniam bonum est in conspe-
ctu sanctorum tuorum·

Dixit insi-
piens in
corde suo:
non est de-
us. Co-
rrupti sunt
et ab homi-
nabiles
facti sunt
in studi-
is suis: non est qui faciat bonum. Do-
minus de celo prospexit super filios homi-
num: ut videat si est intelligens aut requi-
rens deum. Omnes declinaverunt sim-
ul inutiles facti sunt: non est qui faciat bonum non est usque ad unum. Nonne
scient omnes qui operantur iniquitatem:
qui devorant plebem meam ut cibum pa-
nis. Deum non invocaverunt illic tre-
pidaverunt timore: ubi non erat timor·

Polydore Vergil, an Italian scholar who arrived at Henry's court in the latter half of his reign and subsequently lived in England for decades, left this description of the first Tudor monarch:

His body was slender but well built and strong; his height above the average. His appearance was remarkably attractive and his face was cheerful, especially when speaking; his eyes were small and blue, his teeth few, poor and blackish; his hair was thin and white; his complexion sallow. His spirit was distinguished, wise and prudent; his mind was brave and resolute and never, even at moments of the greatest danger, deserted him. He had a most pertinacious memory ... In government he was shrewd and prudent, so that no one dared to get the better of him through deceit or guile. He was gracious and kind and was as attentive to his visitors as he was easy of access. His hospitality was splendidly generous; he was fond of having foreigners at his court and he freely conferred favours of them. But those of his subjects who were indebted to him and who did not pay him due honour or who were generous only with promises, he treated with harsh severity. He well knew how to maintain his royal majesty and all which appertains to kingship at every time and in every place. He was most fortunate in war, although he was constitutionally more inclined to peace than to war. He cherished justice above all things; as a result he vigorously punished violence, manslaughter and every other kind of wickedness whatsoever. Consequently he was greatly regretted on that account by all his subjects, who had been able to conduct their lives peaceably, far removed from the assaults and evil doing of scoundrels. He was the most ardent supporter of our faith, and daily participated with great piety in religious services ... but all these virtues were obscured latterly only by avarice, from which he suffered. This avarice is surely a bad enough vice in a private individual, whom it forever torments; in a monarch indeed it may be considered the worst vice, since it is harmful to everyone, and distorts those qualities of trustfulness, justice and integrity by which the state must be governed.

At court, royal patronage flowed generously to those who had remained loyal to Henry in exile. Henry's stepfather was made Earl of Derby, his uncle Jasper

Opposite: This psalter (prayer book) belonged to Elizabeth of York then Katherine of Aragon. It notes the birth of Henry VII and Elizabeth of York's eldest son, Arthur. At the time, people often noted important family events in their prayer books or Bibles. (Courtesy of Jonathan Reeve JR2153b97plate24 13501400)

SEX IN THE TUDOR ERA

Europeans thought the English were a lusty race and Spanish visitors to London in the 1550s were shocked to see women bare their ankles as they crossed puddles or kiss men on the lips as a form of greeting. Engaged couples were allowed to start having sex with each other before marriage, because their commitment had apparently created a 'pre-contract' of commitment. However, the Tudor parliaments also instituted the first laws which made sex between two adult males a capital crime and one aristocrat, Lord Hungerford, was even executed under the terms of the Buggery Statute. Contraception was rudimentary, with the favourite being the imperfect withdrawal method. Or, as the Tudors colourfully called it, 'hard pissing'.

became Duke of Bedford and married the queen's widowed aunt Katherine, and the Earl of Oxford was given much of the land previously enjoyed by the Howard dukes of Norfolk, who now had to scrape their way back into favour after supporting Richard III at Bosworth. Father Christopher Urswick, who had brought Henry messages from London during his banishment, became Master of King's Hall, Cambridge, and Henry's mother, whose loyalty and devotion had never wavered, became the unofficial first lady of the court. In an era when to walk two to three steps behind royalty was considered a mark of near-unprecedented favour, Margaret was allowed to walk the rather awkward distance of half a step behind Queen Elizabeth, and perhaps unsurprisingly, relations between mother-in-law and daughter-in-law were not always warm. The Spanish ambassador to London joked in his letters to Madrid that, as was always the case, a daughter-in-law chafed at a mother-in-law's dominance.

Things seem to have improved between the two women as the years passed and it was to them, rather than Henry, that the early Tudor court owed its reputation for splendour. Margaret penned a book that laid out the minutiae of royal etiquette and it was adhered to well into the next reign; Elizabeth, who as Edward IV's daughter had grown up at a court praised for its luxury and pomp, helped add a sophisticated lustre to the royal household that it might otherwise have been lacking. And Henry needed these women to help him. What is often overlooked about Henry VII is that he spent the first fourteen years of his life in Wales and the next fourteen in Europe, so in 1485 he found himself king of 'a country he neither knew nor understood.' New palaces arose, with the many-towered riverside wonder at Richmond proving a particular high point of the Renaissance style in northern Europe; the court glittered, its behaviour monitored by the king's mother and its style augmented by his wife. The queen's cousin, the Duke of Buckingham, appeared at state events wearing a sumptuously bejewelled outfit, said to have cost £1,500, at a time when the average weekly wage for a skilled worker was about forty pence and in the period pre-decimalisation of the currency there were 240 pence in every pound. All of the glamour was designed to project an image of a monarchy sedate in its magnificent. Margaret Beaufort and Queen Elizabeth helped create a system which recast a man who had lived life in a kind of shadow as the leading figure in an elaborate political show. The decision to retain many of the advisers who served Henry VI or Edward IV was

Henry VII's daughter and Lady Jane Grey's grandmother, Mary, by an unknown artist. (Courtesy of Jonathan Reeve JR2516b11p7 15001550)

another reflection of the king's conservatism as well as the necessity of having people at his side who actually understood England and the English.

Queen Elizabeth also did her part in steadying the fledgling Tudor dynasty with a flock of children. Part of a medieval queen's duties was to provide for the succession, as Parliament had indelicately reminded Elizabeth at the time of her wedding; through her, 'by the grace of God many hoped there would arise an offspring of the race of Kings for the comfort of the whole realm'. After Arthur's birth, the lovely queen went on to produce six more children – Margaret in 1489, Henry in 1491, Elizabeth in 1492, Edward in 1494, Mary in 1496, Edmund in 1499 and Katherine in 1503.

REBELLIONS

Yet even the queen's fecundity could not completely banish the legacy of generations of infighting; the corpse of the Wars of the Roses kept twitching for the first half of Henry VII's reign. An early uprising against him, led by the who's-who of the what's-left of the Ricardian old guard, ended in ignominious failure, but the threat of deposition hovered over Henry, stoking his increasingly cancerous sense of paranoia. The two most serious threats against him also kicked

Perkin Warbeck. (Courtesy of Jonathan Reeve JRCD3b20p795 14501500)

the hornet's nest of royal control over Ireland, which had been conquered in the twelfth century but which had seen serious fluctuations of loyalty ever since and where the local nobility had been decidedly unenthusiastic about being ruled over by a Welshman. Thus, when a pretender arrived on their shores claiming to be a long-lost prince of the House of York, many of the Anglo-Irish nobles flocked to his banner, including Henry's own lord lieutenant in Ireland, the Earl of Kildare, who helped organise the young man's coronation as 'King Edward VI' in a make-do ceremony at Dublin's Christ Church Cathedral, where he was a crowned with a diadem temporarily borrowed from a nearby statue of Our Lady.

The boy, who claimed to be the Earl of Warwick, Edward IV and Richard III's nephew, was in fact an Oxford joiner's son called Lambert Simnel. The real earl had languished under house arrest in the Tower of London ever since Henry took the crown in 1485, but in an age when pictorial likenesses of royalty, or anyone, were scarce and even then seldom accurate, nobody could tell that the regally dressed chap was nothing more than a mouthpiece for the enterprising tutors and washed-up courtiers who were grooming him. Their forces were defeated, as were those of a later pretender, Perkin Warbeck, who claimed to be the youngest of the vanished Princes in the Tower, who had miraculously escaped and come back to claim his throne. Conscious of the fact that the would-be monarch had been plucked and schooled to play a part in a drama he barely understood, Henry showed leniency and gave Simnel a job in the royal kitchens, turning the spits in the palace's cavernous working fire pits. The adult Warbeck, however, was publicly executed.

Crushing Warbeck greatly increased Henry VII's international standing. To his contemporaries, he had dealt confidently and sensibly with a threat to his rule, and after Warbeck's execution in 1499 Henry was respected as one of the club of Western European monarchs. Spain, newly unified under its co-ruling married sovereigns Ferdinand and Isabella, was pleased to finalise negotiations to marry its monarchs' youngest daughter, Katherine of Aragon, to Henry and Elizabeth's eldest child, Arthur, Prince of Wales. Queen Elizabeth, who was fluent in Spanish, undertook much of the correspondence with Isabella to prepare the Infanta for life in England – part of her advice included familiarising Katherine with wine and weak beer, because in certain parts of London the water was practically undrinkable. Spain demanded the execution of the real Earl of Warwick to prevent any future pretenders as a condition of Katherine's marriage and Henry agreed, in a move which was justifiably condemned by many of his contemporaries. However, the grumbling ceased when the sixteen-year-old Katherine arrived in

England amid scenes of widespread rejoicing, and a lavish public wedding was held at Saint Paul's Cathedral. According to the Spanish ambassador, the king 'much admired her beauty as well as her agreeable and dignified manners'. Tiny in stature, curvaceous and with long blonde hair, Katherine made a favourable impression with almost everyone, but tragedy struck five months into the marriage when young Arthur succumbed to what seems to have been a particularly virulent outbreak of the plague while he and his wife were staying at Ludlow Castle near Wales. The illness was known as the Sweat, a strain of the plague that intermittently swept the British Isles for much of the fifteenth and sixteenth centuries before mysteriously dying out. According to one contemporary, its most

Above left: Katherine of Aragon in middle age. (Courtesy of Ripon Cathedral)

Above right: Her first husband, Arthur Tudor, Prince of Wales. (Courtesy of David Baldwin)

Ludlow Castle, where Katherine of Aragon and Prince Arthur spent their brief marriage. (Courtesy of Elizabeth Norton)

lethal characteristic was its speed, killing 'some within three hours, some within two hours, some merry at dinner and dead at supper'. Princess Katherine was herself deathly ill and had to be moved back to the capital at a snail's pace. Henry was awoken to the terrible news in the middle of his night by his confessor, and the queen arrived to comfort him as he burst into tears. Holding herself together for his sake, she then returned to her own apartments whereupon she fainted and the king was summoned to take care of her.

To preserve the Spanish alliance, plans were made to betroth Katherine to the new heir, Arthur's ten-year-old brother Henry, but the Prince of Wales's death marked the start of the final stage, and dark decline, of Henry VII. Arthur, the golden boy, the apple of his father's eye, was the fourth of the royal children to meet an early death – his sister Elizabeth had died of what seems to have been anaphylactic shock at the age of three, and his two youngest brothers, Edward and Edmund, had died as infants. In 1503, Queen Elizabeth died on her thirty-seventh birthday after giving birth to her eighth child, a daughter, who passed away a week later. According to the up-and-coming lawyer Thomas More, who composed Elizabeth's eulogy, Henry 'privily departed to a solitary place and would no man resort unto him.' Although their marriage had been born of political necessity, he had always been faithful to Elizabeth and her death was sincerely mourned, not just by him but by the wider public, with whom she seems to have enjoyed much popularity. The legend that she inspired the figure of the Queen of Hearts in the traditional pack of playing cards is unlikely to be true, but it gives an idea of the esteem in which so many of her contemporaries held her.

Waning Years

Life within the royal family took a nosedive after Arthur and Elizabeth's deaths. Henry obsessively guarded his new heir with a kind of suffocating protectiveness, while he began to fear that over-exertion in the marriage bed may have hastened Arthur's end. Katherine's claim that the marriage had never been consummated was politely disbelieved by most of the English, and applications to Rome for the Pope to grant a dispensation that would allow Katherine to contravene the teachings of the Book of Leviticus to marry her dead husband's brother fudged the issue, stating that the marriage may or may not have been consummated. After Katherine's mother Queen Isabella died, Henry began to wonder if she was even politically useful to him, slashing her allowance in retribution for her father allegedly failing to pay her full dowry, evading setting a date for her next wedding and making enquiries about the Hapsburg Emperor's granddaughter, the Archduchess Eleanora, as a candidate for young Henry's hand. Uncertainty over her future caused a miserable Katherine to work herself up into a fervour of religious ecstasy and she took to starving herself on fast days with such rigour that even the Pope had to intervene to calm her down, lest it damage her menstrual cycle. She also began complaining of living in poverty, which in relative terms was a slight exaggeration and in real terms an absurdity, but she was certainly miserable and very lonely. The eldest of the Tudor princesses, Margaret, was married to King James IV of Scotland to buy peace along the northern borders, while the king himself briefly considered remarrying to Giovanna, the buxom Dowager Queen of the Naples, although nothing came of that or of plans to marry his son to Eleanora of Austria.

Paranoid about money, Henry relied more and more on legally dubious means to extort cash from his subjects and after limiting their abilities to retain soldiers,

Henry VII (top) and Henry VIII; political art stressed the continuity of the family line. (Courtesy of Elizabeth Norton)

something he not unfairly blamed for the longevity of the Wars of the Roses, he also began levelling punitive fines on the nobility, which he would only partially collect and then would hold like the sword of Damocles over their heads, guaranteeing their continued obedience. The aging king and his councillors pursued every avenue of his fiscal rights, squeezing all the money they could from his unhappy subjects, and in doing so they pushed the letter of the law to its limits. Indeed, if Thomas More is to be believed, they went beyond it. The councillors he appointed to carry out his unpopular new fiscal policies, men like Richard Empson and Edmund Dudley, had previously made a reputation for themselves in the House of Commons, but they earned nationwide detestation for being so closely associated with Henry's long winter of tax hikes. The waspish conclusion of one modern writer, that Henry's 'incessant money-grabbing was frankly rather middle-class', pales in comparison to contemporary rage, with one aristocratic lady lambasting the government for its 'malicious enmity and false craft' against the people. Worn out by tuberculosis, Henry VII passed away in his beautiful Richmond Palace on 28 April 1509 after a reign of twenty-four years and at the age of fifty-two. As he lay dying, he asked his confessors to grant him pardon for his greed.

At the time of his death, when he was conveyed to his heart-stoppingly beautiful golden sepulchre at Westminster to lie alongside the remains of his queen, Henry was, in the words of an Italian visitor, 'feared rather than loved'. This was not true in his native Wales, where his upending of the penal legislation that had reduced the Welsh people's legal rights in comparison to the English ensured that he was eulogised by a Welsh bard as 'a Moses who delivered us from our bondage', but perhaps the Elizabethan Francis Bacon's assessment of Henry VII as Solomon, a wise ruler who asked far too much of his people, remains the fairest assessment of the first Tudor sovereign. He had ended the military strife that plagued his parents' generation; he had survived numerous attempts to depose him; he had left the Crown solvent for the first time in years; his son's was the first undisputed accession in England since 1422 and under his rule his kingdom had become wealthier, safer and internationally respected. Against this, however, was his avarice, which, like his dishonesty and suspiciousness, got worse as he grew older. Polydore Vergil's aforementioned judgement that greed 'is harmful to everyone, and distorts those qualities of trustfulness, justice and integrity by which the state must be governed' captured the essential failure amid a life of great success for the Welsh fugitive who became king against impossible odds and gave peace to his people, but who died largely unloved.

3

HENRY VIII: 'VIRTUE, GLORY AND IMMORTALITY'?

Henry VIII was born on 28 June 1491, the third of Henry VII and Elizabeth of York's children and their second son. At the age of three, his father made him Duke of York, a deliberate elevation that was designed to disassociate the title with the numerous pretenders claiming to be one of Elizabeth's long-lost brothers. The majority of his childhood was spent at the pretty riverside palace at Eltham, where he and his sisters were cared for by a sizeable retinue of servants, since custom at the time tried to remove royal children from the claustrophobic stench of the cities; Queen Elizabeth was a constant presence in her younger children's lives, even if the king naturally focussed most of his attention on the Prince of Wales. Still, Henry received an excellent education and when the visiting philosopher Erasmus of Rotterdam was brought to meet the royal children during his visit to England, he seemed particularly struck by the younger boy's precocity.

Arthur's death in 1502 made Henry heir apparent, and he inherited not just his dead brother's titles as Prince of Wales and Duke of Cornwall, but also his widow. Henry VII's feet-dragging over the marriage of the new heir to the princess dowager is notorious (and has been dealt with in a previous chapter); while he lived the young pair's future was in limbo. Then in 1509, Henry VII was dead, leaving the throne and a sizeable treasury to his seventeen-year-old son.

A NEW CAMELOT

The outburst of rejoicing which greeted the new king reflected the country's relief that after nearly a century the monarchy had returned to the stability which, as an institution, it was supposed to guarantee, but it was also caused in no small part by the six-foot-two monarch's appearance – golden hair, muscular frame and all the towering good looks of the York kings from whom he descended on his mother's side. He was the reborn sun, recalling his grandfather Edward IV, the famously good-looking 'sun in splendour', banishing the shadow of Henry

VII's increasingly unpopular government. For the first few years of his reign, no superlative seemed excessive in describing Henry VIII. The Venetian ambassador thought he was 'extremely handsome' and waxed lyrical on how, when the king played tennis, he was mesmerised by the sight of 'his fair skin glowing through a shirt of the finest texture'. He was considered 'much handsomer than any sovereign in Christendom; a great deal handsomer than the King of France, very fair and his whole frame admirably proportioned'. A courtier, Lord Mountjoy, enthused, 'everything is full of milk and honey and nectar. Avarice has fled the country. Our King is not after gold, or gems, or precious metals, but virtue, glory, immortality.'

Yet even here, in the halcyon days surrounding his accession, there were ominous indicators of what he was capable of, precursors of what was to come; Henry ordered the executions of Richard Empson and Edmund Dudley. The two men had languished in the Tower ever since their master's death, and as they were the councillors most clearly associated with Henry VII's unpopular taxes, their executions greatly increased the young king's already considerable popularity. But the evidence against them was dubious at best, the legal procedures enacted to bring them to the scaffold oppressive and brisk; everything they had done they had done at the behest of Henry VIII's father, but they paid for that with their lives.

Like most children of repressively strict parents, Henry VIII went wild with his newfound freedom. His coronation was lavish and the court went from the dour days of Henry VII's decline to a seemingly unending sequence of jousts, entertainments, pageants and feasts, in which the young king stood centre stage as the star attraction, a role he relished. One of the chief beneficiaries of the regime change was Katherine of Aragon, who became Henry's wife within a few weeks of his accession. Camelot needed a queen and a troubadour needed his lady. Whether Henry VIII really was in love with her, as generations of romantics have claimed thanks to his titling of himself as Katherine's 'Sir Loyal Heart' in the jousts, is difficult to ascertain. Hyperbole was an integral part of courtly love, the politics of display which sought to ally outrageous flirting with an Arthurian ideal of kingship. Katherine may have been very pretty, impeccably well behaved and very popular, but we have no way of knowing what Henry actually felt about her beyond his extravagant declarations of devotion during court entertainments. Certainly, he was unfaithful to her almost from the start; an intrigue with one of the Duke of Buckingham's sisters humiliated the queen and enraged the duke, who felt it was a slight on the family's honour. Contrary to what is suggested in many of today's romantic bestsellers, most aristocratic families in the sixteenth century saw the kingly seduction of their women as a deep insult, since every subsequent promotion for the clan would be put down to the woman's immorality rather than the menfolk's achievements. Greed does not always trump pride. Queen Katherine learned her lesson after her futile fury over the affair ended with one of her favourite ladies-in-waiting being banished from court as a punishment, and so she never again voiced an objection to her husband's philandering, turning a blind eye both to her own heartache and her role as guardian of the girls' honour when the king came sniffing around some of her maids.

The first decade of the reign was marked by prodigious spending. It was not so much the decadence of the court, itself considerable, which caused the greatest damage. Even if Queen Katherine wrote to her father in Spain, 'Our time is passed in continual feasts', a few parties were hardly likely to bankrupt the nation. Rather, the real damage was done by the wars which Henry, hungry for glory, embarked upon with his French neighbours. These achieved almost nothing save their cost, and perhaps the most important long-term development

An Allegory of the Tudor Succession showing Henry VIII and his children, all three of whom succeeded him. The portrait was painted in Elizabeth's time, so she is shown flanked by the figures of Peace and Plenty, while her sister Mary is accompanied by her Spanish husband and the figure of War. (Courtesy of Yale Center for British Art, Paul Mellon Collection)

from the French campaigns was the ascent of Father Thomas Wolsey, a brilliant Oxford graduate who set to work with the zealous efficiency of a big business banker mixed with a ruthless bureaucrat to organise and finance every detail of the invasion. As a result, he became indispensable to Henry, who was bored by minutiae of government but still felt confident in directing the bigger picture, and Wolsey rose through the bishoprics to become Lord Chancellor, a cardinal and the king's right-hand man. By the end of the 1510s, he was the most powerful lay man in England, after the king, and the most powerful cleric bar none. Hampton Court Palace, originally built for him, is a tribute to his extraordinary wealth and equally impressive confidence.

As with all powerful men, Cardinal Wolsey made enemies for himself. In the first place, the queen, having had a taste of tangible political influence in the first five years of the reign, gradually saw herself eclipsed by the cardinal and undermined when her father's slippery behaviour made the Spanish alliance seem more trouble than it was worth. Wolsey also ticked off aristocratic grandees, chief among them the king's second cousin, the Duke of Buckingham, who thought it obscene that the son of a butcher from Ipswich could have more say in government than nobles, and he also enraged prominent aristocratic families like the Boleyns when he blocked too many aristocratic promotions and instituted sweeping reforms of the royal household which saw many of them lose their lucrative jobs at the king's side. He was blamed for the Duke of Buckingham's arrest and execution in 1521, although the king had feared his proud and charismatic cousin for years.

At the same time as the duke's downfall, the royal marriage was beginning to give cause for concern. A string of pregnancies had ravaged the queen's figure, but there was still no heir. Her first pregnancy in 1510 turned out to be a phantom, with the queen's hysteria rearing its head as she insisted on taking to her birthing chamber despite the physicians' uncertainty over how genuine her condition actually was. As was customary, the queen was conducted to a sealed-off set of apartments, devoid of male company, for a month preceding the birth. She was cut off from most forms of natural light bar one small window, insulated from harmful odours in the outside air and kept that way until after the birth, when she was churched – a religious ceremony designed to purify her from the stain of childbirth, the burden all women had inherited from Eve. In 1510, Katherine's time in the pseudo-purdah of confinement produced nothing but a discreetly covered-up embarrassment. Thankfully, she was legitimately pregnant within a few months. A son, the hoped-for heir, was born in 1511, but died six weeks later while the country was still celebrating his arrival. Katherine was devastated and

Right: Henry VIII's most prominent mistress, Elizabeth Blount, from a carving on her parents' tomb. (Courtesy of Elizabeth Norton)

Below: Henry VII, Henry VIII and Archbishop Cranmer in a stained-glass window in Canterbury Catheral. (Courtesy of Amy Licence)

made 'much lamentation' according to a contemporary. Her ensuing catalogue of miscarriages and stillbirths tormented her, until she produced the couple's only surviving child, the future Queen Mary I, who was born at Greenwich Palace in February 1516. The king added insult to injury by fathering a healthy bastard son via his most prominent early mistress, Elizabeth Blount, a gorgeous and vivacious young woman whom he apparently noticed when they danced together in a masquerade at Christmas 1514. In 1519, shortly after Queen Katherine's final pregnancy, Blount gave birth to a boy who was christened Henry FitzRoy ('son of the King'), whom Henry proudly acknowledged as his own. The child was the much-needed proof of his virility, and was eventually given a splendid establishment of his own and created a duke twice over.

RIVAL QUEENS

As Katherine of Aragon worried about the possibility of her child being shunted to one side to make way for FitzRoy and the nobility fidgeted at the faint rumours of a bastard inheritance, the world outside England began to change rapidly as the anti-establishment protests of German ex-monk Martin Luther put the flame into the kindling of a continent-wide dissatisfaction at the corruption of the papacy, which had become the plaything of dubious Mediterranean families like the Borgias and the Medicis. A genuine hunger for spiritual renewal collided with political unrest to create, to the surprise of almost everyone involved, a new kind of Christianity – Protestantism – and the shattering of centuries of theological certainty. Henry was initially repulsed by Martin Luther's demands, penning a book so extravagant in its defence of the Pope's prerogatives that a grateful pontiff declared Henry *Fidei Defensor*, Defender of the Faith, a title still borne by Henry's modern-day successors. Soon, all these threads – the stagnation of the royal marriage, aristocratic resentment against Cardinal Wolsey, the looming crisis over the succession and a continent in the flux of the Reformation – wove together in the career of Henry's second wife, Anne Boleyn.

She burst on to the court's social life with the rather appropriate pseudonym of Lady Perseverance, a role she was given in an extravagant celebratory masque along with six other of the court's most celebrated women, including the king's youngest sister and his cousin's wife, Gertrude, Marchioness of Exeter. Anne had been educated on the Continent, shipped off to the Hapsburg court thanks to her father's honey-voiced *diplomatesse*, and from there to the household of the French royal family, where she acquired her fluency in the language and a

Henry VIII's controversial and glamorous second wife
Anne Boleyn, in one of many copies of an original which
has since vanished. (Courtesy of Ripon Cathedral)

cosmopolitan gloss that never quite left her. Exotic, exquisitely well mannered, charismatic and with a razor-sharp sense of humour, she had beautiful dark eyes, an elegant figure and a flair for fashion. Stories of six fingers on her left hand, third nipples and strawberry-shaped moles on her neck are mentioned in none of the eyewitness accounts and date from a hostile Catholic propaganda tract from the 1570s, which also claimed she was secretly Henry VIII's biological daughter and a witch. In Paris, they thought she was very beautiful, a Cambridge don said 'competent belle' ('quite beautiful') and an Italian diplomat described her as 'not one of the handsomest women in the world'. The only portrait of her which does seem to tally with descriptions of her appearance, although it is a later copy, shows a thin young brunette wearing the famous pearl and gold 'B' pendant and clutching a rose. There are so many variations of this lady, with slight alterations to her hair colour, hands and outfit, that the most likely explanation is that they are all copies inspired by a now-lost original from her lifetime.

She returned to England in 1521 or early in 1522, and her family secured her a place in the household of Queen Katherine. One quote claimed later that she 'sang like a second Orpheus, she would have made bears and wolves attentive', and this, coupled with her skills as a dancer and aristocratic French manners, helped explain her rise in the court's popularity stakes to win the role in the *Château Vert* masque in 1522. Her family had briefly considered marrying her to her Irish cousin, the future Earl of Kildare, and later she had apparently fallen in love with the Earl of Northumberland's heir to the extent that there had been talk of marriage.

Dating Henry's own pursuit of Anne is difficult, with some, like Cardinal Wolsey's usher George Cavendish, suggesting that it began at the same time as her romance with the future Lord Northumberland, which, if true, would place the king's interest in her almost to the time of her court debut in 1522. However, confusion over Anne's early career at the English court is rife, even in the relatively contemporary sources. All that can be said with any degree of certainty was that Henry was writing love letters to her in 1527. Anne famously refused his many attempts to make her his mistress, but her moves to escape his attentions were often confused and faintly panicked, far from the cool self-aware genius she is usually accredited with. A loss of virginity outside of wedlock, even if it was to someone like the king, would make her soiled goods on the marriage market, and Anne was ambitious enough to want to marry well – her previous two potential husbands had both been future earls, all her maternal aunts had married earls and her father was heir presumptive to the Irish earldom of Ormond. But what may simply have been sensible pragmatism about the *modus operandi* of aristocratic marriages struck Henry VIII as an expression of Anne's commendable moral scruples and, who knows, it may have been just that – we know almost nothing about Anne Boleyn's state of mind in 1527, since only Henry's side of their early correspondence survives, housed, with the supreme irony that history loves, in the Vatican archives.

Anne's behaviour, flitting between obvious flattery at such prolonged attention from the king and reticence about what it could do to her reputation, inflamed Henry's ardour and coincided, though she can hardly have known it, with Henry and Wolsey's doubts about the future of the royal marriage. Then, either in late 1527 or early 1528, Henry proposed to Anne. After some hesitation, she agreed by sending him a jewel showing a young maiden seeking shelter in a storm-tossed ship. The road ahead would be difficult, but Anne had agreed to make the journey at Henry's side.

But Lady Perseverance was a role that could equally belong to Queen Katherine,

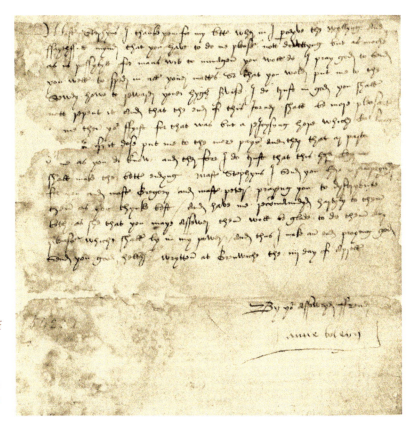

Letter from Anne Boleyn to Stephen Gardiner, the future Bishop of Winchester, on 4 April 1529. (Courtesy of Jonathan Reeve JR964b20p900 15001600)

because once she got wind of the government's plans to annul her marriage on the grounds that her previous marriage to Henry's brother had been consummated and her subsequent match was thus incestuous, she rose to the challenge of defending it with a tenacity that can only be described as magnificent. She fought her husband every step of the way. She acquired allies in the clergy, supporters in foreign universities, sought help from her relatives in Europe and defied a papal legate, Cardinal Campeggio, who had been sent to England to mediate between the couple and tried to persuade Katherine to solve the problem by voluntarily retiring to a nunnery like Louis XII of France's late wife, the saintly Jeanne de Valois, who had stepped aside to make way for his remarriage to the more fecund Anne of Brittany. Katherine would not budge and in 1529, at a public hearing held with Cardinals Wolsey and Campeggio supervising, she made a superb and emotive defence of her marriage, shredding the government's argument that the couple had been cursed with childlessness (or sonlessness, as Henry insisted) because of the sinful nature of marrying your husband's brother: 'By me ye have had divers [many] children, although it hath pleased God to call them from this world.'

Katherine's refusal to back down caused a headache for the Pope, especially when she invoked the help of her Hapsburg relatives, who were arguably the most powerful family in the world at the time and certainly the most influential in the Italian peninsula. The Pope, the weak and corrupt Guilio de Medici who had become Clement VII, could not afford to offend them, which is why Cardinal Campeggio was under strict instructions to get Katherine to step aside. However, Katherine's vigour was not the only reason why Clement could not annul her marriage; he was also put in a very difficult position thanks to Henry VIII's heavy-handed negotiating tactics. Nearly every move Henry VIII made over the course of his first divorce, the 'Great Matter', was the wrong one and he, as much as Katherine, bears responsibility for the seven-year mess and numerous ruined careers.

The first major political casualty was Cardinal Wolsey, who was dismissed and died in disgrace after his failure to fix this greatest of Henry's problems. Another Lord Chancellor, the devout Thomas More, resigned when he became unhappy at the rising prominence of Protestant-sympathisers at court, and in 1532 Anne Boleyn scored a major victory by having a friend of the family, the Cambridge don Thomas Cranmer, appointed Archbishop of Canterbury. By that stage, Katherine had been separated from her only daughter and banished to internal exile, where once again her claims of suffering the pains of Purgatory on earth thanks to her newfound poverty struck a slightly over-the-top note. At court, the queen-to-be was surrounded by people who gave her books that rubbished papal

Above: Cardinal Wolsey in his last days at Leicester Abbey, 1530. (Courtesy of Jonathan Reeve JR1094b20fp904 15001550)

Right: Thomas Cranmer, the first Protestant Archbishop of Canterbury, by Gerlach Flicke. (Courtesy of Elizabeth Norton)

authority, and she in her turn passed them onto the king, helpfully pointing out the most relevant passages. Parliamentary pressure was brought to bear on the clergy; Archbishop Cranmer declared the marriage between Henry and Katherine invalid, bastardised their horrified sixteen-year-old daughter in the process and sometime in late 1532 or early 1533 Henry and Anne were privately married. It is not true that they took this step because Anne was pregnant; she did not give birth until September, so the numbers quite simply do not add up. It is quite possible, and even probable, that they both abstained from sexual relations until

A lavish triumphal archway designed for Anne Boleyn's coronation procession through London. (Courtesy of Elizabeth Norton)

the ring was safely on Anne's finger. As the summer sun rose on an England now hurtling towards a full break with the Roman Catholic Church, a sumptuously dressed Anne was processed through the capital to her own glittering coronation at Westminster Abbey, where every detail of the ancient medieval ceremony was adhered to, as if nothing had changed.

It was a dazzling illusion, because the Reformation and break with Rome unleashed a tsunami of political and cultural change that swept over England for the next two generations. Rising to fill the gap left by Cardinal Wolsey was his one-time secretary Thomas Cromwell, another commoner with a flair for organisation, who became the Henrician Reformation's henchman, initiating a parliamentary campaign against the monasteries by closing them down and pouring their wealth into the king's coffers, while organising the dozens of trials and executions of those who refused to accept that Henry, once Defender of the Faith, was now Supreme Head of the Church in the Holy Father's place. Thomas More and Cardinal Fisher, a brilliant scholar, were the most high-profile victims of the cull and they both met their deaths with exemplary bravery, although More's critics pointed out that his bravery was no less than that of the Protestants he had condemned to death in the flames during his time as Lord Chancellor.

THE DOWNFALL OF ANNE BOLEYN

The queen, who lifted not one finger to help More or Fisher, increasingly squirmed at the rapacity the royal commissioners were showing as they ransacked the monasteries. Anne had always taken her vocation as a queen consort, saturated with images of the Virgin Mary and Esther, the Old Testament's virtuous heroine queen, seriously, and Thomas Cromwell's machinations sat uneasily with both her desire to be liked and her insistence on micromanaging those around her. It said something for her chutzpah that she launched herself in a courtly battle with Cromwell, likening him to Haman, Esther's corrupt and would-be genocidal nemesis, even as her own position as Henry's beloved weakened. Her first pregnancy had resulted in the birth of a daughter, Elizabeth, and there had been at least one subsequent miscarriage. The king had returned to his old womanising ways and at a state dinner the French ambassador noticed how unsettled the queen was by her husband's philandering. Then, to the general astonishment of Europe, on 19 May 1536 Anne became the first queen in English history to be publicly executed. Two days earlier, five men were executed for being her adulterous lovers, including her brother, Lord Rochford. One of the victims, a

Above: Wolsey dismissed by Henry VIII. A Victorian reconstruction. (Courtesy of Jonathan Reeve JR1092b20fp896 15001550)

Left: Sir Thomas More. (Courtesy of Elizabeth Norton)

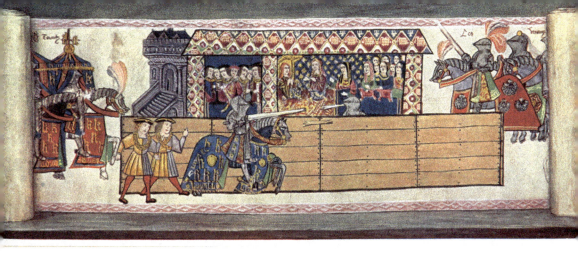

Jousting was a popular but highly dangerous pastime at the Tudor courts. (Courtesy of Jonathan Reeve, JR1098b2fp204 15001550)

palace musician called Mark Smeaton, had either been tortured or threatened with it. A fellow palace servant heard later that he had been 'grievously racked'.

Explaining how Anne Boleyn became the Tudor court's Guinevere has excited scholars for years, resulting in an academic spat in the usually more sedate pages of the *English Historical Review* in the early 1990s, prompting the Oxford historian Steve Gunn to quip that the debate over Anne's downfall constituted 'academic trench warfare'. The easiest explanation, and one adhered to by Henry's enthusiastic nineteenth-century admirers, who saw him as one of the British Empire's founding fathers, was that Anne must have been guilty. Otherwise their hero would never have behaved so terribly towards her. This view looks increasingly untenable when set alongside the fact that there were over a dozen errors in the indictments against Anne, in which she or her alleged lovers were nowhere near the place they were alleged to have had sex in. A variation of this argument was resurrected in 1991 by George W. Bernard and then again in his 2010 biography of Anne; he argued that although many of the charges against Anne seem preposterous and it is unlikely that she committed incest or adultery with all five, 'it remains my hunch that Anne had indeed committed adultery with Norris, probably with Smeaton, possibly with Weston, and was then the victim of the most appalling bad luck'. But while Anne was shaking with terror and suffering erratic mood swings in her rooms at the Tower, her behaviour before her judges was calm, with the Hapsburgs' ambassador complimenting her answers, saying that she rebutted all the charges against her very convincingly. Shortly before dying, she proclaimed her innocence at one final Mass. The king's own joyous behaviour, which included banqueting and feasting in night-time river

Jane Seymour.
(Courtesy of Stephen Porter)

parties on the Thames while the queen was imprisoned, strikes a suspicious note if compared to his humiliated fury when he genuinely believed that his fifth wife, Catherine Howard, had taken a lover a few years later.

A theory put forward in the 1980s by Professor Retha M. Warnicke argued that Anne's final miscarriage in January 1536 held the key because the foetus had been partially deformed, which resulted in the queen being suspected of witchcraft and those around her, including her homosexual brother Lord Rochford and his lover Mark Smeaton, of being sexual deviants who had consorted with the queen in other 'unnatural' activities, resulting in the monstrous birth. However, there is very little evidence to support the idea that George Boleyn, Lord Rochford was a homosexual, and almost nothing in way of concrete evidence to clinch the idea that the king and queen's child in 1536 was somehow deformed. The historian Greg Walker does not believe Anne was guilty, but thinks her flirtatious nature gave credibility to the charges against her. The most popular theory, put forward by the late and much-missed Eric Ives, and expanded on by others, is that Anne's death 'is explained by what happened not in the bedroom, but in the corridors of power'. In this version of events, she was the victim of a coup, with Thomas Cromwell moving to destroy her before she could attack him and striking down some of her most influential supporters by accusing them of being her lovers, then selecting a suitably weak and malleable servant like Mark Smeaton who could be tortured into providing the necessary fig leaf of legal evidence needed to begin the arrests. Finally, and perhaps most chillingly of all, is the conclusion of two of the king's modern biographers, J. J. Scarisbrick and Derek Wilson, which holds that Henry knew his wife was innocent, wanted rid of her and allowed Cromwell to organise the case against her once his own obsessive, possessive fascination with Anne finally ended, as it so often does in the most tragic of cases, when 'devastating infatuation had turned into bloodthirsty loathing, for reasons we will never completely know'. The 'extremely cumbersome and illegal means … used to bring Anne down' somehow whiff of Henry's own cumbersome attempts to secure his first divorce, putting him at the centre of what happened in 1536, not Thomas Cromwell.

Whatever happened – and with the destruction of so many of the original documents in an accidental library fire in the eighteenth century we may never know – Anne met her death bravely according to the eyewitnesses, and eleven days later Henry married the dignified and enigmatic Jane Seymour. His third marriage coincided with a massive rebellion against the closure of the monasteries in the North, which Henry defeated by inviting the leaders to court, promising change, granting amnesty, then having them executed the minute they went home

Left: The badge of Jane Seymour. (Courtesy of Elizabeth Norton)

Below left: Anne of Cleves. (Courtesy of Jonathan Reeve JR 822b53fp414 15001550)

Below right: Henry's fifth wife, Catherine Howard, dressed as the Queen of Sheba. (Courtesy of Elizabeth Norton)

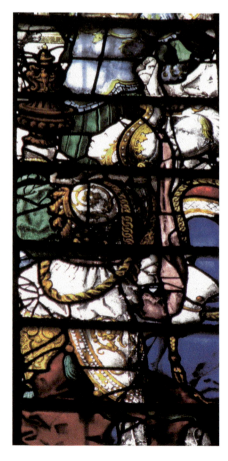

HENRY VIII: A SYPHILITIC KING?

The story that Henry VIII suffered from syphilis did the rounds in the sixteenth century and the Internet has breathed new life into it, but there is no truth in it. In the first place, he exhibited almost no signs of the disease which, in the sixteenth century, would have been difficult to hide, especially as the disease reached its horrifying conclusion. Secondly, syphilis was a new phenomenon in Europe in the 1500s, because it was carried back to the Continent by the sailors who discovered the New World. It was therefore a notorious illness that was usually treated with mercury in an expensive and painful procedure. However, we know from Henry VIII's meticulous medical records that he never received any mercury treatments. So, no syphilis, but he did suffer from an agonising pus-filled leg ulcer after a fall from his horse in 1536, gout and, perhaps needless to say, many health problems associated with obesity. By the end of his life, he was so fat that his servants had to lift him by a small crane on to what must have been a very sturdy horse.

and instituting a policy of mass repression on the region. The new queen died on 24 October 1537, twelve days after giving birth to Henry's heir, Prince Edward, who took precedence over his sisters Mary and Elizabeth, both disinherited, and replaced his bastard brother, the Duke of Richmond, who had died either of tuberculosis or during an outbreak of the plague a year earlier.

THE FINAL DECADE OF HENRY VIII

Henry remained single for two and a half years, as the princesses of Europe all found excuses to reject his proposals. Pride of place for putdowns goes to the Dowager Duchess of Milan, who quipped she would need two heads to feel safe in marrying Henry. As he grew older, muscle turned to fat as the king gorged himself at meals, swelling to an enormous size. The court artist, Hans Holbein, managed to rebrand this as impressive majesty in his looming and unforgettable portraits that show Henry, magnificently dressed, codpiece jutting forward and feet astride, master of his universe. Middle age also brought a swing, as it does for so many, in the conservative direction and the king began to look at the burgeoning number of independent Protestant denominations with unease. To him, their insistence on interpreting the Bible for themselves stank of heresy. At the same time, the great Catholic powers of Europe, France and the Hapsburg Empire, were lining up against him, using his repudiation of the Pope as an excuse to strike, and in January 1540 Cromwell persuaded the king to marry Anne of Cleves, the twenty-four-year-old sister of a German duke who was head of a cabal of princelings committed to undermining the power of the Hapsburgs. The marriage was a six-month fiasco, and not just because France and the Hapsburgs went back to fighting each other before they could attack England. On the wedding night, Henry claimed he could not sustain an erection in Anne's presence (leading to subsequent theories that he may have suffered from intermittent erectile dysfunction in old age), and six months later she was packed off to the English countryside with a staggeringly generous divorce package after she sensibly co-operated fully with the king, who could not quite believe his luck compared to how wives numbers one and two had taken their impending demotions. Two weeks after the divorce, a disgraced Cromwell was beheaded on charges of heresy and treason, a few of his fellow Protestants were consigned to the flames at Smithfield and Henry married Catherine Howard, the lovely orphaned niece of the Duke of Norfolk, whose glee at Cromwell's downfall was faintly unsettling to behold. The queen was young enough to be her husband's granddaughter by contemporary standards.

In the summer of 1541, the year after his marriage to the teenaged Catherine, Henry toured the north of England to solidify royal control over the region after the rebellion. Before he set off on the progress, he ordered the execution of the elderly Countess of Salisbury, his mother's cousin, who was awoken in her cell at the Tower, told she had an hour to live and then dragged to her execution, where an inexperienced executioner hacked her to pieces with an inexpertly wielded axe. Her faint claim to throne and children's opposition to the break with Rome sealed her fate. Nine months later, the flagstones above her grave in the Tower of London were disturbed to make way for Queen Catherine Howard, sent to the block with a favourite lady-in-waiting after a love letter from her to a handsome courtier condemned them all to death. The lady-in-waiting perished for arranging the meetings.

Personal humiliation for the aging and bloated monarch was soothed by the defeat of an invading Scottish army at Solway Moss, in a loss so catastrophic that it hastened the nervous breakdown and eventual death of King James V of Scotland, who was succeeded by his six-day-old daughter Mary, Queen of Scots, whom Henry now set about trying to capture to force into marriage with his own son, thus uniting

Katherine Parr, Henry VIII's last wife. (Courtesy of Elizabeth Norton)

Henry VIII in later life. From a boxwood carving at Sudeley Castle. (Courtesy of Jonathan Reeve JR2600b120fp158 15001550)

the kingdoms in a personal union. As the Tudor forces attacked their country, the Scots wryly nicknamed it 'the Rough Wooing' and Mary's widowed mother got her safely out of the country to her relatives in France, where she spent the rest of her childhood. In Ireland, the Dublin parliament voted through the Crown of Ireland Act, which elevated the monarch's title from Lord of Ireland to King of Ireland, and in July of the following year Katherine Parr, a thirty-year-old widow with a passion for theological debate, became the first queen consort of Ireland when she married the king, not entirely enthusiastically, in a ceremony at Hampton Court.

She was at his side when the threat of invasion by the French saw the capsizing of the prized warship *Mary Rose*. Katherine Parr's fervent Protestant faith very nearly got her into serious trouble, and Henry was not above hanging the threat of arrest over her until she learned to stop questioning him. With theatrical subservience, the queen threw herself at her husband's feet and proclaimed that as a woman she only argued in his presence so she could have the privilege of hearing his counterpoints. As faction reigned unchecked in the increasingly vicious corridors of power, and the religious question became the dominant dividing factor, Henry tried to draw up a will that would prevent one clique from triumphing over the other once he was gone. But as his health declined, he was more and more a plaything in the hands of his intimate servants, at least one of whom, Sir Anthony Denny (who had the job of Groom of the Stool, that is, the gentleman who accompanied the king to the toilet), was firmly on the side of the reformers, and when Henry passed away on 28 January 1547, they were able to delay the announcement long enough to surround the nine-year-old King Edward VI with men sympathetic to their cause and have his Seymour uncle, Edward, proclaimed Lord Protector, regent in effect, until the boy came of age.

Henry was buried next to Jane Seymour in Saint George's Chapel at Windsor. Years later, a romantic story arose claiming he chose to lie next to her because she was the only wife he had ever really loved, but he could hardly have rested next to the wives he had divorced and executed, or Katherine Parr, who was childless and still alive. As far as he and most of his contemporaries were concerned, Queen Jane, the mother of the new king, had been Henry's only truly successful consort. Henry had always planned to erect a magnificent tomb, a testament to his glory, but his children did not inherit the same kind of money as he had done. Instead they got a debased coinage, rampant inflation and a foreign policy in tatters. No one could afford to finish Henry VIII's monument. In the end all his dreams of glory were replaced by an underwhelming inconsequentiality – a plain black stone with his name and the year of his death.

4

EDWARD VI: 'A SPIRIT OF CAPACITY'

Henry VIII's will left the crown to his son Edward. If Edward died without heirs, the throne should pass to his much older sister Mary, Katherine of Aragon's daughter, and if she died in a childless state, Henry wanted her to be succeeded by Anne Boleyn's only surviving child, Elizabeth. If, in her turn, Elizabeth passed away without heirs, the royal inheritance was to go to the descendants of Henry VIII's youngest sister Mary, Duchess of Suffolk, who had married an English nobleman and whose daughters had since likewise married into the kingdom. If the Suffolk line failed then, and only then, was the crown to pass to the descendants of Henry's eldest sister, the late Margaret, Queen Mother of Scotland, whose granddaughter Mary, Queen of Scots, never accepted that her great-uncle had any right to wreak havoc with the laws of primogeniture, which clearly stipulated that the eldest daughter's line should take precedence over the youngest's. If the two countries were to be united, Henry wanted it with England's royal line doing the deed, not Scotland's.

Those squabbles seemed a distant possibility in 1547 with the coronation of the nine-year-old Edward VI. With his grey eyes, pursed lips and pale complexion, he strongly resembled his mother, Queen Jane Seymour, whom he had lost within days of being born after the royal physicians, anxious for their share of the glory, excluded experienced midwives from the prince's birth and accidentally allowed parts of the placenta to remain in the queen's womb, resulting in an agonising series of haemorrhages and quite probably sceptic shock, which killed her on 24 October 1537. From the beginning of his time as king, the half-Seymour Edward was surrounded by his mother's kin. His uncle Edward Seymour, Earl of Hertford, was quick, ambitious and cerebral. He began his career at Henry VIII's court by serving as a pageboy in the household of the king's youngest sister and skilfully acted as a chaperone to his own sister Jane once she became the object of the king's affections. He held on to royal favour and expanded his influence after Jane's death, no mean achievement, and in 1547 he moved with lightning efficiency to make himself de facto ruler of the realm while his nephew remained a child.

Edward Prince of Wales.

Edward VI by
Hans Holbein.
(Courtesy of
Stephen Porter)

THE BOY KING'S GUARDIANS

Edward Seymour's power chafed his younger brother, the adventurous and reckless Thomas, who caused a scandal by eloping with Henry VIII's charming widow, Katherine Parr, only a few months after the old king's funeral. Edward promoted himself through two more rungs of the English aristocracy's hierarchy to make himself Duke of Somerset, while Thomas had to content himself with being Baron Sudeley. Duke was the highest title available, baron was the lowest, and the dashing Thomas felt the humiliation keenly. In 1548, his wife died in childbirth and an almighty ruckus erupted when she accused him on her deathbed of making inappropriate advances to the king's teenage sister Elizabeth, who had lived in Katherine's care since King Henry's death. Rumour suggested that Thomas Seymour had also made overtures of marriage to Princess Mary, the heiress apparent, and even to Henry VIII's wealthy ex-wife, Anne of Cleves. Fearing that the scandal over his relationship with Elizabeth would allow his enemies at court to destroy him and consumed by envy for his eldest brother, Thomas Seymour smuggled himself into his nephew's apartments at Westminster and began giving him money, as well as advice that he ought to free himself from his other uncle's influence. Matters came to a head when stress and mounting self-doubt caused Thomas to panic on finding the king's door bolted one night; he shot the sovereign's beloved barking dog and thus provided enough evidence, just about, for him to be charged with treason and the attempted kidnapping of the king. Edward Seymour presided over his younger brother's downfall with a chilling indifference or, as he might have seen it, commendably impartial rectitude. Thomas Seymour was beheaded on 20 March 1549 and it was said later that Elizabeth Tudor, the precocious young girl he had tried to force his attentions on, remarked that a man of much wit but very little judgement had died that day. Whether she actually said it or not, it was a fitting epitaph for Thomas Seymour.

Thirteen at the time of his uncle's execution, Edward VI, like his cousin Jane, had an intelligence that bordered on the genius. His biographer Dale Hoak has convincingly argued that the young man's memory may have been photographic, illustrated by the fact that he could remember ever creek, bay and rivulet in England, Scotland and France, and at the age of nine had memorised four books by the Roman philosopher, Cato. Thanks to a rigorous education in classics, theology, linguistics, literature, mathematics and history, which saw the child taught Greek by the Regius professor at Cambridge, Edward built on his own natural intellect to develop an extraordinary mind. One of his tutors, Dr Richard Cox, made a grand understatement when he described his charge as having a 'towardness in learning' and 'a spirit of capacity'. As king, Edward also loved to hunt, joust, practise his sword fighting and exercise. Despite his gravity and preternatural self-control when in public, he did have close relationships with boys his own age, including Barnaby Fitzpatrick, the eldest son of an Irish baron, who had joined Edward's schoolroom and became a lifelong friend.

A PROTESTANT JOSIAH

Most of Edward's tutors had been strongly sympathetic to the Reformation and this trend of surrounding himself with Protestants continued after his accession. Edward's Archbishop of Canterbury, Anne Boleyn's one-time dependent Thomas Cranmer, felt far more comfortable showing his true theological colours once Henry VIII was safely dead. He urged the new king to carry the Reformation to its logical conclusion by eradicating the last signs of Catholic worship. What followed was the evisceration of England and Wales's churches, and the brutal destruction of nearly a millennia of their artistic heritage amid a deluge of whitewashing paint brushes, ham-fisted vandals and unshakable theological self-righteousness. The next in line to the throne, Edward's devout sister Mary, was appalled and blamed the king's advisers, despite the fact that her polite protestations that the king was too young to fully understand what his government was doing were undercut by Edward's eye-wateringly rude public lectures to her, in which he mocked the Mass she cherished and upbraided her for daring to hold religious views contrary to her king and master's. All of it ringing down through the centuries with the voice of an incorrigible prig.

But that was not entirely his fault. Edward was constantly in the company of men who had given themselves over completely to the mission of the Reformation, and many of them quite sincerely believed in the rhetoric which cast Edward as a latter-day Josiah, the Old Testament boy king who had cast down idolatry and restored true religion to his people. Candles were removed from churches, along with stained-glass windows, religious icons, statues and carvings. Processions were banned, as were maypoles, for good measure, Purgatory was declared a nonsense, Latin was struck from the services, and prayers for the dead, redundant once Purgatory was non-existent, were prohibited. Archbishop Cranmer's new Book of Common Prayer sought to impose Protestant uniformity on English worship, and while today it is a beloved bastion of spiritual conservatism in the British Isles, in the 1540s its prose struck many of Edward VI's subjects as alien, radical and objectionable. It collided with growing agrarian unrest, sustained inflation inherited from Henry VIII, massive government borrowing, the unpopularity of the Lord Protector, expensive wars with Scotland and France, again caused in no small part by lingering resentment in those countries at the legacy of Henry VIII's foreign policy, and parliamentary criticism of the king's advisers. All these factors produced a series of enormous rebellions, in which there were so many casualties that, to give an idea to the modern reader, if the 1549 uprisings took place today, proportionally adjusted for the country's population, the equivalent death toll would have been about 200,000. His opponents on the council struck against Edward Seymour, who was removed from office, accused of treason and met the same fate as his brother. Like Thomas, he tried to hold on to power by holding on to the king, but he lost his nephew's support when he bungled him off to Windsor Castle, where Edward caught a fever and icily complained that the castle had not been made ready for his residence, likening his stay there to being in 'prison'.

The coronation procession of Edward VI in 1547. (Courtesy of Jonathan Reeve JR1167b4p710 15501600)

Edward Seymour was soon replaced by another ambitious career courtier, John Dudley, who had worked hard to overcome the stain on the family's name left when his father Edmund was executed by Henry VIII in 1510 after years of faithful service to Henry VII. In the long run, the younger Dudley was to prove no more popular with the people of England than his father, and many began to look back favourably on the dead Edward Seymour, retrospectively referring to him as 'The Good Duke' in contrast to Dudley, 'The Bad Duke'. Having been in charge of Queen Catherine Howard's horses and married to one of her ladies-in-waiting, Dudley subsequently worked his way into the council and from there helped lead the coup against the Seymour faction, making himself Duke of Northumberland afterwards. Realising that Edward would legally come of age eventually, Northumberland was clever enough to allow Edward VI a greater sense of independence than he had enjoyed under the care of his late uncle, and the court, residing in the fifty-five splendid homes it had inherited from the acquisitive

Henry VIII, developed more of a character that was distinctly to Edward's liking. One suspects that not every courtier was thrilled at the required attendance to the three-to-four-hour-long sermons Edward liked to listen to from his favourite preachers, but at least there were also masquerades and jousts to distract them, coupled with the king's love of finery, high expenditure on glittering jewels to augment his majesty and an adherence to the lovely details of etiquette which drew admiring compliments from the usually contemptuous rival court in Paris.

Despite his reputation for out-of-control ambition and total self-promotion,

HELPING THE POOR

Medieval Catholic institutions like the monasteries and poorhouses had traditionally provided help to the nation's poor, so after their destruction the government had to work on new ways to alleviate poverty. The royal family, pre- and post-Reformation, were particularly well-organised in their generosity, even adhering to the old medieval ritual of washing the feet of local paupers on Maundy Thursday, in imitation of Christ's actions at the Last Supper. More long-term plans were put in place under Elizabeth I's government, which were sorely lacking by modern standards, but which lasted as legislation until the nineteenth century.

Northumberland did try to moderate some of the king's more extreme religious policies, particularly when his continued bullying of his eldest sister culminated in an international crisis via a threat from her cousin, the Hapsburg Emperor Charles V, that he would intervene in English affairs if the princess was not allowed to hear Mass in private. Talk of the king's own future marriage began to dominate gossip at court and meetings of the council. When he was a child, his father had wanted to marry him to Mary, Queen of Scots, thus uniting England and Scotland, but the Scottish queen was now safely in France and preparing to marry the heir to its throne. Edward's uncle Thomas had promoted the idea of Edward marrying one of his own subjects, his second cousin Lady Jane Grey, who shared Edward's passion for books and Protestantism in equal measure. Edward, who wanted a match worthy of his station and none of his father's romantic wanderlust, was receptive to proposals that he help heal the rift between the two countries by marrying the king of France's eldest daughter, Elisabeth. Since the French royal family would never have countenanced Elisabeth's conversion from Catholicism, it raises the possibility that Edward was becoming more flexible, by a margin, than he had been as a boy.

Safeguarding the Succession

All these plans for the future and the reformers' hopes for a Protestant commonwealth led by one of their own came to naught. In March 1553, a diplomat visiting London from Venice met Edward and wrote home that the King of England was a very handsome young man, but quite clearly dying. A variety of theories have been put forward to explain why this apparently healthy young man died before his sixteenth birthday. Renal failure, tuberculosis and measles, which left him fatally weak to secondary infections, have all been suggested. Realising that death was rapidly closing in on him, Edward writhed in agony at the thought of leaving his kingdom to his Catholic sister. He could skip over her to bequeath the crown to Elizabeth, who was a Protestant, although a far less fiery one than Edward, but the legal justification for doing so was practically non-existent. It was not until the seventeenth century that a British monarch's religious faith became a criterion for their succession. In 1553, it would have struck many people as absurd to move past the eldest sister in favour of the younger, as reactions to Henry VIII's convoluted and contested will made clear. Edward was also privately unconvinced that either Mary or Elizabeth should wear the crown, since both had been declared illegitimate by their father. They were acknowledged as Henry VIII's biological daughters, but born from illegal unions with two mothers who had both failed at queenship. He removed them both from the succession and moved to the next line stipulated by his father's will: Lady Jane Grey was the eldest granddaughter of Henry VIII's younger sister and her English husband, and she had also just been married to Northumberland's son Guildford, which ensured the duke was actively promoting her candidacy. She was a zealous Protestant, whose reputation was above reproach and whose world view corresponded closely to Edward's. When some of the assembled courtiers, summoned to hear their king's dying wishes as his frame approached the skeletal, voiced concerns over how Mary's disinheritance would play with the public, Edward rebuked them with 'sharp words and angry countenance'.

On 6 July 1553, the fifteen-year-old died at Greenwich Palace in the arms of two of his childhood friends, praying that his device to make Jane Dudley England's first queen regnant and its second truly Protestant monarch would work.

5

QUEEN JANE: 'A TIME TO BE BORN, AND A TIME TO DIE'

When they hacked off Jane Dudley's head on 12 February 1554, one eyewitness wrote later that the spectators were surprised to see so much blood gush forth from such a small body. The young lady had exited the mortal plain in a way which would have made her cousin King Edward very proud: she had been offered her life on the condition she converted to Catholicism, but she refused. The image of Jane, blindfolded and reaching out her arms towards the block, panicking in shattered calm when she could not find it, was arresting – an unforgettable vignette of uncertain youth in a cruel situation. It stayed in the collective imagination, helping to fuel the nineteenth century's particular obsession with her. To the Victorians, Jane Grey (they preferred to remember her by her maiden name) was the apotheosis of the pure young maiden, the damsel in distress, almost a virgin sacrifice on the altar of pernicious politics. Paul Delaroche's magnificent painting of Jane's execution dates from 1833 and it shows Jane, garbed entirely in white, lurching towards the block while prostrate ladies-in-waiting weep behind her.

Fascination with Jane's purity and her suffering amounted almost to a cultural fetish. In a letter to Evelyn Waugh, the genius responsible for *Brideshead Revisited*, the socialite Nancy Mitford remembered, 'I used to masturbate whenever I thought about Lady Jane Grey, so I thought about her almost continually and even executed a fine watercolour of her on the scaffold ... I still get quite excited when I think of Lady Jane (less and less often as the years roll on).' Mitford loved an anecdote, the more outrageous the better, but on a more restrained level Jane stood alongside Mary, Queen of Scots, and Marie-Antoinette as polite Victorian and Edwardian society's ideal of the ultimate lady brought low by tragedy and the sordid actions of others. Yet this version of Jane as a pious young bluestocking ultimately helped erase the real girl's fire, and the public's interest in Jane reached such an intensity that contemporary accounts of her life and death, purporting to be genuine, were in fact manufactured in the 1800s and taken as fact until they were only, very recently, disproved.

Jane's date of birth was once given as October 1537, making her almost exactly of

Lady Jane Grey. (Courtesy of Elizabeth Norton)

an age with Edward VI, but recent research suggests that she was more probably born a few months earlier, perhaps in the early summer. Her father Henry Grey was the Marquess of Dorset and descended from Henry VIII's grandmother, Queen Elizabeth Woodville, but it was her mother's blood which really mattered, particularly as the Anglo-Irish nobilities tended to put as much stock in the maternal inheritance as they did the paternal. Jane's mother, Frances Grey (*née* Brandon), was the eldest surviving child and heiress of Henry VIII's best friend Charles Brandon, Duke of Suffolk, and the king's youngest sister, Mary. Through Frances, Henry Grey enjoyed the uxorial title of Duke of Suffolk after his father-in-law's death in 1545 and Jane grew up splitting her time between Bradgate, her family's enormous estate in Leicestershire, now a picturesque ruin, and the royal household's establishments in the south, where her mother somehow managed with magical tact to remain on equally good terms with all members of the dysfunctional reigning family. Her parents ensured that Jane and her two younger sisters, Catherine, a statuesque beauty, and Mary, who may have had dwarfism, received an excellent education. Despite the duke and duchess's best efforts, no son survived to inherit their joined titles. In time, it looked as if it might all pass to Jane and, through her, to her eventual husband.

AN UNHAPPY CHILDHOOD?

Sending one's child to be raised as a ward with a prestigious relative or benefactor was a common part of aristocratic upbringing in the sixteenth century: Anne Boleyn had been sent to the care of the Archduchess Margaret of Austria while still a very young girl, and Catherine Howard spent most of her childhood with her grandmother, the Dowager Duchess of Norfolk. As she grew, Jane was sent to join the household of her great-uncle's sixth wife, Queen Katherine Parr. The religious view of Jane's parents already leaned strongly towards Protestantism, but it was in Queen Katherine's company that Jane really embraced the new faith with a zeal that was to play a part in ending her life so prematurely. The queen was an enthusiastic convert, a born-again evangelical who had written her own prayer books that all expressed an unashamedly Protestant theology. Jane remained in Katherine's care even after the latter was widowed and remarried to Thomas Seymour in 1547. Seymour soon reached out to young Jane's parents, persuading them to join in his schemes to place himself closer to the new monarch; their incentive was Seymour's promise to promote Jane as a candidate for Edward's hand in marriage. That plan imploded with Katherine Parr's death in childbed – Jane acted as a chief mourner in her elaborate funeral – and then with Thomas Seymour's subsequent execution for treason.

Jane returned to her parents' household, where the scholar Roger Ascham encountered her reading the works of the Greek philosopher Plato while her parents and their guests had gone hunting. Jane complained about how little her parents understood her true personality, telling Ascham, a sympathetic audience if ever there was one, that she would much rather be left to her books than cajoled into physical activities. This meeting, which Ascham recorded almost verbatim, led to posterity dismissing Jane's mother and father as abusive philistines, but Jane was going through nothing more dramatic than adolescent angst. What teenager has not complained of being misunderstood? And how many parents, before and since, have nagged said budding adult to get some fresh air and a bit of exercise? Her parents had provided Jane and her sisters with a curriculum that left all of them, and Jane in particular, extremely bright and well-read. They can hardly therefore fairly stand accused of being hostile to culture and learning.

There were other signs of decidedly self-righteous and even bratty behaviour from Jane, including mortifying rudeness when her parents decided to spend a few days at the country house of Frances's cousin, Princess Mary. When Jane spotted one of the princess's Catholic ladies-in-waiting genuflecting before the Consecrated Host, the blessed communion bread which Catholics believe becomes the spiritual Body of Christ and which Protestants in contrast interpret purely as symbolic, she asked why the lady was curtseying, even though she must surely have known the answer as the debate over transubstantiation was the burning issue of the day, quite literally, and Jane was fascinated with theological texts. The lady stiffly replied that she was kneeling to her maker, to which Jane quipped that she may as well curtsey to the baker because he had made the bread and that was all the host amounted to.

THE NINE-DAY QUEEN

There is not much evidence to suggest that Edward VI ever seriously considered marrying Jane after his uncle Thomas's death, but even the prospect of seeing Elisabeth de Valois as the next queen of England and Ireland evaporated once it became clear that the king was dying in early 1553. The Duke of Northumberland, fearful of losing power if Princess Mary succeeded to the throne, reached out to Jane's parents with a solution that would enable them to step even closer to the centre of power and preserve the Protestant settlement established by Edward. Frances would renounce her own blood claim to the crown to pass it directly to her eldest daughter, who would marry one of Northumberland's unmarried sons. In return, Northumberland would facilitate Jane's accession instead of Mary's. Dazzled at the prospect opening up before them and swiftly abandoning their former friendship with Mary Tudor, the Suffolks arranged Jane's marriage to Northumberland's son, Lord Guildford Dudley, at Durham House in London on 25 May 1553.

Although her marriage was later presented as a miserable one, perhaps due to the ruthless politics which motivated its creation, there is little in the contemporary sources that backs this up. When she was asked to stand as godmother to one of her guard's children and given the customary honour of selecting the baby's name, Jane chose Guildford, and shortly before her execution she turned down her husband's request that they meet one last time, because an emotional reunion might rattle the dignity with which they must greet their deaths. All of this indicates an amicable, and perhaps even a loving, relationship. In any case, she had been raised like all noble girls to know that one day she would marry a man of her parents' choosing and that she must, as an obedient daughter, accept their decision.

Jane was, however, initially far more reticent at the prospect of becoming the country's first queen regnant. The capital shared her ambivalence, with the crowds greeting the proclamations of her accession with hostile silence. A young apprentice boy called Gilbert Potter had his ears cut off for crying out his support for Princess Mary. Northumberland also had to work hard to persuade his colleagues on the council to support his new daughter-in-law's succession. From her countryside estates in the north, Princess Mary rallied the people to her banners to be borne towards London on a crest of popular acclamation, as crowds gathered in their thousands to uphold the social hierarchy. Mary arrived in the city to near-universal acclaim, flanked by her younger sister Elizabeth, in a show of sibling solidarity, and by Anne of Cleves, keen to show her loyalty to the new regime to ensure the payments she had been promised in her divorce settlement from Henry VIII were still honoured. Jane, Guildford and their rapidly dwindling entourage had sought refuge in the Tower where, like sitting ducks, they were transformed from a court into prisoners as Jane's tenure as monarch collapsed nine days after her accession.

DEATH FOR PROTESTANTISM

Mary I was initially prepared to show leniency towards the men and women who had tried to disinherit her, with the exception of the Duke of Northumberland, whom she loathed, and who had seemingly been the chief architect of the plot. He was executed and several of his loyal sons joined their brother Guildford in the Tower. However, while they were condemned as traitors, Jane, her husband and her parents were allowed to live, even if Jane's actions during the dying days

The signing of the death warrant of Lady Jane Grey. Engraved by Charles Burt *c.* 1848. (Courtesy of the Library of Congress)

of her rule, when she tried to encourage people to fight for her cause against Mary's approaching army, suggested that she had been just as determined in the end to keep a Catholic from the throne. Housed in comfortable rooms in the Tower, which had once been a royal palace, Jane's fate was sealed when her father foolishly became involved in a rebellion and the Spanish ambassador bluntly told Queen Mary that her proposed marriage to Prince Philip of Spain could not go ahead if she continued to allow such a serious threat as Jane Dudley to remain alive. Mary recoiled at the idea of executing her cousin and dispatched Father John Feckenham, a learned and gentle Catholic priest with an impressive track record in scoring conversions. His mission was to offer Jane her life in return for her commitment to the Catholic faith. If she did that, then the threat was neutralised; if she did not, then it was no longer Mary's fault if she perished. Jane saw Feckenham, and the queen's offer, as a temptation sent directly from the Devil to jeopardise her immortal soul by embracing a religion which she had once referred to as 'the stinking and filthy kennel of Satan'. Throughout their long debates, she refused to budge and even valiantly attempted to convert him to her religion, paying tribute to Feckenham's eloquence as she did so: 'I pray God, in the bowels of His mercy, to send you His Holy Spirit; for He hath given you his great gift of utterance, if it pleased Him also to open the eyes of your heart.'

In her final few days, she wrote letters to her young sisters urging them not to curry favour with the queen by converting to Catholicism, and to her father, in which she forgave him for his foolhardy actions in leading a rebellion which caused his daughter's execution. She submitted herself to medical examinations to prove she was not pregnant, which might have stayed the execution by a few months. Through it all, she comforted herself with thoughts of Heaven and God's inestimable mercy: 'For as the Preacher says, there is a time to be born, and a time to die; and the day of death is better than the day of our birth.' On 12 February 1554, Guildford was beheaded first and Jane, whose name he may have carved on the walls of his rooms, was led, a tiny figure in a dark dress, out on to the courtyard of the Tower, where she recited the Psalms and spoke kindly to a distraught Feckenham, who had asked to be allowed to accompany her. Her final speech implicitly rinsed the Catholic doctrine of Purgatory by expressly requesting prayers only for as long as she was alive, because Protestants held to the belief that one's salvation was decided upon by God and could not be influenced after death. Then, she was blinded and helped towards the block, when she found she was kneeling too far away from it. The axe sliced through her neck, producing a torrent of blood from the seventeen-year-old.

The London skyline, taken from a painting by Claes Visscher, 1616. The Tower of London looms on the left. (Courtesy of Stephen Porter)

6

MARY I: 'IN GOOD FAITH'

Despite her seeming reluctance at signing Jane Dudley's death warrant, the fact was that within a year of taking the throne Mary I's attitude towards dissent had already hardened. Jane's body was barely cold before Mary's younger sister and heiress apparent Elizabeth was winging her way towards the Tower after the queen suspected her of complicity in a rebellion against her, which had arisen in Kent but made its way to the gates of the capital before it was defeated. Its leader, Sir Thomas Wyatt the Younger, insisted that their main objective had been to prevent the queen's impending marriage to her second cousin, Prince Philip of Spain, not to overthrow her. Mary did not believe them and neither did many of her advisers. There was a slew of executions, including that of Jane Grey's father; the marriage to Philip went ahead at Winchester Cathedral and Elizabeth only escaped the scaffold by stubbornly clinging to her story that she had known absolutely nothing about Wyatt's treasonous enterprise.

PRINCESS FROM A BROKEN HOME

Marriage with a Hapsburg had been on the cards for Mary Tudor almost from birth. Her mother, Katherine of Aragon, had dreamed of a match for her with Mary's first cousin, Charles V, who inherited the Spanish throne as well as being elected emperor of the central European empire of the Hapsburgs to become the most powerful man in Christendom. That match fell through when Charles, tiring of the alliance and disinclined to wait until Mary reached maturity, jilted her for Isabella of Portugal in 1526, when Mary was ten years old. Charles and Mary remained close, however, with Charles becoming a distant surrogate father figure in Mary's eyes when her own tore her pampered childhood asunder to initiate annulment proceedings against her mother. Ironically, had Katherine of Aragon acquiesced to the divorce in its early stages she could have preserved Mary's place in the line of succession, because the Church allowed children to remain legitimate

MARIA : REGINA

Mary I. (Courtesy of Ripon Cathedral)

if they were conceived 'in good faith', meaning when two people joined together in an illegal union but had not yet realised it, which, according to Henry VIII, was what had happened with Mary. In trying to save her own title, Queen Katherine unintentionally helped destroy her daughter's and Mary was declared a bastard once the annulment was finally announced by means other than papal approval in the spring of 1533.

Separated from her mother from the age of fourteen, Mary was not allowed to see her even when she fell ill with increasing frequency and severity for the rest of the decade. She had inherited her hysterical temperament from her mother and, worse, her father's tendency to hypochondria. In Mary, physical pain all too often manifested itself alongside severe emotional distress. Mary's new stepmother, Anne Boleyn, set out to win the girl's friendship, deploying every weapon in her arsenal and holding forth the glittering temptation that she would be restored to the heart of the royal family, treated as the queen's favourite at court, and once again put in charge of a lavish household with numerous servants of her own, if only she would accept the validity of the Great Divorce. At the same time, Katherine of Aragon was writing to Mary, urging her to put her head on the executioner's block rather than accept the new Church of England or, through it, Anne's queenship. When Mary and Anne Boleyn attended a Mass together, one of Anne's ladies-in-waiting saw Mary curtseying and thought she was making an obeisance to Anne. She reported this gesture to the queen, who was overjoyed and sent a messenger profusely apologising for missing it, assuring Mary that Anne would now speak to the king personally to end Mary's rustication from court. Mary replied that she had been genuflecting to the altar, not Anne, adding that she acknowledged no queen in England bar Katherine and referred to Anne as the king's mistress. Afterwards, Queen Anne twisted etiquette like a knife edge into the ex-princess's flesh, insisting that Mary, now forced to live as a lodger in the massive household given to Anne's toddler daughter Elizabeth, be treated as Elizabeth's subordinate at all times. Piqued, Mary refused to eat and her health deteriorated as a result, on top of which she began suffering what would now probably be recognised as rolling cycles of depression.

Even Anne Boleyn's execution in 1536 did not bring an end to Mary's unhappiness. Despite her supporters' insistence that it had all been the Boleyn queen's fault, pressure on Mary to accept her father's control over the Church actually increased after Anne's death. Even the new and allegedly sympathetic queen, Jane Seymour, did nothing to help until Mary, surrounded on all sides and missing her mother's stiffening courage ever since the latter's death from cancer, finally gave in and swore painful vows acknowledging her own illegitimacy and the dissolution of papal authority in England. She was received back at court, where both King Henry and Queen Jane made a great fuss over her, insisting that nothing gave them greater pleasure than Mary's return and acting as if the last five years had all been a strange, inexplicable, faultless blip. The Duke of Norfolk said that if he had a daughter who had behaved as stubbornly as Mary, he would have beaten her until her head resembled a soft apple. Mary, however, regarded herself as disgustingly weak and wrote in secret to Rome, begging the Pontiff to secretly absolve her of obedience to the hateful oaths she had just publicly taken.

For the rest of her father's reign, she alternated between her estates in the countryside and residency at court. She was not pretty, but she had the red Tudor hair and pale skin, with a deep and almost masculine voice of her own. She was a dapper dresser with a great interest in fashion, a love of jewels and a reckless gambling streak, she enjoyed music and had fluency in English, Latin and Spanish, as well as a solid working grasp of Italian. She got on very well with Anne of Cleves, who was only six months her senior, quarrelled with Catherine Howard and enjoyed a close friendship with Katherine Parr, which soured when Mary felt propriety had been outraged by Katherine's swift elopement with Thomas Seymour so soon after Henry VIII's funeral.

THE RESTORATION OF CATHOLICISM

Mary's unhappiness at the religious changes made by her brother's government has already been mentioned, but Mary certainly felt more comfortable opposing him than their father. Even so, Edward VI's displeasure and Mary's distrust of those who advised him resulted in at least one spell when Mary quite seriously considered fleeing England to start a new life in the reassuringly Catholic Hapsburg Empire, under the protection of her cousin, the emperor. It was only when some of her devoted servants pointed out that if she left the kingdom she forfeited her chance to inherit it one day that Mary finally buried the plans and rose, like a proud Fury, to sweep south on London when Jane Grey was declared queen in her place.

A year into her rule and Mary felt the first chill winds of doubt; her accession had not brought the universal return to the old religion or the total obedience she had expected. Her imprisonment of Elizabeth in the Tower soured relations between the sisters, which only worsened when a put-upon Elizabeth went through a theatrically reluctant conversion to Catholicism to appease the queen, who now seemed to equate Protestantism with treason thanks to Wyatt's uprising. Catholicism had

The burning of Bishop John Hooper at Gloucester, 9 February 1555, from Foxe's *Book of Martyrs*. (Courtesy of Jonathan Reeve JRCD2b20p1004 15501600)

DEATH BY BURNING

Death by flame is one of the era's most notorious punishments, first introduced into England by the pious King Henry IV in the fifteenth century as punishment for heresy, holding opinions which violated the core teachings of the Church. As an act of mercy, the victims were sometimes given a small bag of gunpowder to tie around themselves, so that they would die quicker. Damp wood was a particular fear, since it could greatly prolong the agony of the condemned. One particularly memorable death took place at Oxford in 1555 when Thomas Cranmer, the ex-archbishop of Canterbury, thrust one of his hands into the flames. It was the hand he had used to sign documents accepting Mary I's Catholic government.

always been a mainstay of Mary's life, her great consolation and the constant she clung to amid deteriorating relationships with her father and brother, but she could not, or would not, appreciate that some people could feel the same way about Protestantism. She abolished the Church of England, resubmitted her kingdoms to Vatican authority, and reinstituted legislation from the time of Henry IV which made heresy a crime punishable by burning. Hundreds were arrested, and nearly 300 met their deaths in the flames, including Edward VI's aged Archbishop of Canterbury, who was also Princess Elizabeth's godfather. High-ranking Protestants became refugees, many seeking temporary asylum in the Protestant republic in Geneva, and while most ordinary English people had been ambivalent or even hostile to the Protestant Reformation when it first began, the bravery of the martyrs as they faced their deaths generated much sympathy for their cause.

Mary's marriage to the son of her cousin the emperor was not popular, even with some of her councillors. There were fisticuffs between some of the English courtiers and the Spanish arrivals, mirroring the country's general distrust of the union. Philip, who became King Philip II when his pious father abdicated to spend the rest of his life in contemplation at a monastery, was charming and courteous, but he was also ambitious and incapable of overcoming England's entrenched xenophobia, which fed on fears that the queen's marriage would suck England into permanent dependence on the Hapsburg Empire. Despite her adoration of him, Mary herself seemed supportive of Parliament's attempts to deny Philip the Crown Matrimonial,

Mary I's husband, King Philip II of Spain. (Courtesy of Jonathan Reeve JR188b4p823 15001600)

whereby he could potentially enjoy kingly powers by virtue of his marriage to the queen. Wives were supposed to be utterly subservient to their husbands, but neither Parliament nor Mary were keen to see their monarchy incorporated into Philip's.

Mary's two pregnancies were yet further humiliations for her husband; one lasted for fourteen months and both proved phantoms, in a mirror of Mary's late mother's behaviour four decades earlier. The king began to spend more time away from England, visiting his vast continental dominions and smarting from Parliament's hostility towards him; Elizabeth, distancing herself from the regime and as unhappy with Mary's actions as Mary had once been at Edward's, increasingly figured in Mary's nightmares as the secretly Protestant successor-in-the-wings. Capable of magnificent moments of rhetoric when addressing her subjects, as her triumphal entry into London at the start of her reign had shown, Mary was slowly wounded by her phantom pregnancies, her husband's absence, her diminishing popularity and by the horror of the French armies retaking the port of Calais, England's only remaining continental possession, after Mary entered a war against France as part of the key terms of honouring her alliance with the Hapsburgs. The loss, which devastated the queen, only increased the people's hostility towards her husband.

A Blood-Soaked Queen?

There has long been a suspicion that Mary's final alleged pregnancy was in fact a mistaken diagnosis of the ovarian cancer which ultimately killed her, although Linda Porter, one of Mary's most recent biographers, has suggested that she may have succumbed to a particularly virulent influenza outbreak that left her fatally weak. Her relationship with Elizabeth was now marred by corrosive suspicion and, on Mary's part, equally corrosive nastiness. When he was trying to disinherit her, Edward VI had made sweepingly judgemental comments about Anne Boleyn's execution for adultery as proof of Elizabeth's unsuitability for the throne. Mary went a step further when, in a particularly foul mood, she claimed that Elizabeth was not really her sister because she physically resembled Mark Smeaton, one of the men executed for being Anne Boleyn's lover. This accusation has rung down through the centuries, leaving a question mark over Elizabeth's paternity for those inclined to believe the worst or the most scandalous rumours, of which there are many in history. But what is often overlooked is that Mary could not possibly have known what Mark Smeaton actually looked like, because he only came to court shortly before she left it and even then he started out as a minor singer in the household of Cardinal Wolsey, not of the king, the queen or the Princess Mary. By the time Smeaton joined the royal household, she was languishing in internal exile and by the time she came back, he was dead. Mary's slur on her sister was thus nothing more than a cruel and bad-tempered exploitation of the circumstances that had robbed Elizabeth of her mother.

At her country palace at Hatfield, a regal Elizabeth watched with disgust as courtiers arrived to do homage to her, abandoning an ailing Mary in London. Elizabeth was pragmatic enough to accept their loyalty as she prepared to assume the throne, but she never forgot the unsavoury sight of rats fleeing the sinking ship. She griped that it was a particular failure in mankind, and especially in the English, that they worshipped the rising sun more than the one setting. She remembered it when her own time came half a century later.

In October 1558, Mary heard that her cousin Charles V had passed away and by November her own end was rapidly approaching. She died on 17 November at Saint James's Palace, while hearing Mass and surrounded by her ladies-in-waiting. She gave a shudder at the moment of the Elevation of the Host, the central Catholic mystery of faith which Edward VI and Jane Grey had once so ridiculed and in the defence of which Mary had consigned nearly 300 people to the flames. It was a near-saintly death for a pious lady, who had shown through her defence of her royal prerogatives that a woman could rule in her own right, but whose attempted restoration of Catholicism, although very popular with thousands of her subjects, had made her many enemies through the Protestants' public martyrdoms. Her bungled foreign policy had lost Calais, which may have been of minimal financial or tactical use, but it had had huge symbolic importance as the last remnant of England's once vast European empire. Mary, no less than her subjects, felt its loss keenly. In years to come, Mary was roundly demonised by the triumphant Protestants as 'Bloody Mary', with influential Protestant histories depicting her as a depraved and cruel monster. Some 130 years after her death, Britain's last Catholic monarch was overthrown in part because of the collective cultural neuroses that Mary I's legacy still caused. A Catholic sovereign had become inextricably linked with the fear of tyranny. While Jane Grey was immortalised in paint as Delaroche's virginal-pure martyr, in 2010 the London Dungeons advertised their tours with a poster showing a portrait of Mary morphing into a blood-drinking zombie. If historians still debate the success or otherwise of Mary I's government, the dark legend of Bloody Mary is unlikely to lose its hold for many years to come.

7

ELIZABETH I: 'ONE MISTRESS, AND NO MASTER'

Elizabeth I's coronation was a difficult experience for her ladies-in-waiting, some of whom were almost toppled over by the crowd's frenzied enthusiasm for the new monarch – moments after the twenty-five-year-old queen walked past they tore up the blue velvet carpet that lined her way from Westminster Abbey, making it tough for the people who had to follow in her wake. The spectators' adoration was a testament to Elizabeth Tudor's inimitable flair for public relations; she had an unfailing ability to do and say the right thing in public, which enabled her to work a crowd with a charisma that made her father and sister appear staid in comparison. She spoke to her subjects with all the passion reserved for the love of one's life and, for the girl who lost her mother before her third birthday and had grown to maturity knowing only a distant and capricious father, it was safe to say that the people's enthusiasm for her was reciprocal. At the end of her life she told a group of her subjects, 'There is no jewel, be it of never so rich a price, which I set before this jewel: I mean your love. For I do esteem it more than any treasure or riches; for that we know how to prize, but love and thanks I count invaluable. And, though God hath raised me high, yet this I count the glory of my Crown, that I have reigned with your loves.'

QUEENS AND SPECULATION

Elizabeth was not beautiful, but she was striking – 'handsome' was a word tossed around by several observers in her younger days – and her appearance was a visible blend of her immediate forebears: she had the high Boleyn cheekbones and a small, expressive mouth, with the long Tudor face and Beaufort nose, which the more charitably souled could describe as distinguished. Her colouring was Yorkist – a flawless pale complexion and fair-to-red hair, and her build, luckily for her given her father's late-in-life *embonpoint*, was that of the slender Howard women from whom her mother descended. Her eyes, like her mother's, were dark

Hatfield House, the childhood home of Elizabeth I. (Courtesy of Elizabeth Norton)

and expressive. Her education, entrusted by her doting mother to a set of reliably loyal governesses to whom Elizabeth remained devoted for the rest of her life, soon expanded to the rigorous Renaissance curriculum later experienced by her younger brother and cousin, Lady Jane Grey. By the time she was eleven, Elizabeth was penning letters in Italian to her stepmother and translating prayer books from French into English; she acquired fluency in French, Latin, Italian and Greek, along with a working knowledge of Spanish, Portuguese, German and Welsh. Her favourite mode of relaxation was to translate works of Roman philosophy from Latin into English and then back again, to see how well she had done the first time round. Like most of her family, she loved music, played well and danced better. Most of her tutors were sympathetic to the New Religion and when she became queen in 1558, this svelte and brilliant young woman instantly became the most desired catch in Europe, particularly, but not exclusively, for Protestant royalty. There was no shortage of suitors; even her former brother-in-law, the devoutly Catholic King Philip II of Spain, expressed an interest, much to Elizabeth's thinly

ELIZABETA dei gra. Regina Angliæ, Franciæ & Hiberniæ
fidei Defensor. & cetera Potentiss: principi D: Ferdinando, diuina clementia
fauente, electo Romanorum Imperatori semper Augusto. ac Germaniæ,
Hungariæ, Bohemiæ, Dalmatiæ, Croatiæ, Sclauoniæ & cetera Regi, fratri
et consanguineo nostro charissimo salutem in dno. Accepimus lras vestras
quas 27 Februarij ad nos scriptas, Legatus et Consiliarius vr Georgius Comes
in Helffensteyn attulit, quibus nos valdè amanter et beneuolè hortata est
Ser.tas vestra vt eidem Legato vro, fidem adhiberemus. Quod quu lrarum
partim fuerat, propter Ser. vræ authoritatem concedere, tum certè propter Legati
vri prudentia et humanitatem, maximè verò om propter earu reru, quas nobis idem
Legatus vr exposuit, dignitatem, æquissimo aio eu audiuimus. Cuius ex sermone, studium & beneuolentia vram, multis testimonijs declarata, verbóque
sacro Imperatoris confirmatu, erga nos plenè perspeximus, eamq nulla in re
erga nos inferiorem, quàm erga Chariss: sorore nostra Reginam Mariam
iam defunctam, (quanq vre Ser: paulò propinqiore) existere intelligimus.
Pro hac Ser. vrę tam perspicua animi propensione, gras et nuc quàm max.as
libenter agimus, et quandocunq occasio tulerit, ot officij ratione, nostram quoq
gratificandi voluntatem, sedulo et abundè declarabimus. Atq hunc nostrę
beneuolentię sensu, ex sermone Legati vri, cui, quantu Ser vrę debeamus,
prolixe exposuimus, plenius quàm ex nostris hijs lris Ser.tas vra intelliget. Deus
Ser vram, ad Eccliam Catholica foeliciter propagandam, ad sacrum Imperij
fortiter sustentandu, ad dignitatem vram abundè amplificanda diu conseruet.
DAT: in Regia nostra Westmon, quinto die Martij. M: D: LVIIIo.

Vestræ Serenitatis Soror & Consanguinea

Elizabeth

veiled disgust. There were offers from Archduke Charles of Austria and King Eric XIV of Sweden. In the 1570s, Elizabeth underwent a semi-public gynaecological examination to prove she was fit to bear children if her proposed marriage to the Duc d'Anjou, the French king's youngest brother, went ahead.

The problem was that Elizabeth openly expressed her preference to, in her own words, 'live and die a virgin'. The tragic fate of her mother and third stepmother, Catherine Howard, had left deep emotional wounds and childhood friends recalled that it was shortly after Catherine's execution in 1542 that the eight-year-old Elizabeth made her first promise that she would never marry. As she blossomed into adulthood, her stepfather Thomas Seymour, a handsome and dashing man, made advances that left her a confusing mixture of flattered, mortified and afraid. When he began to enter her bedroom in the morning under the pretext of tickling her, while wearing nothing but his night shirt, Elizabeth took to getting up hours earlier so that she could already be fully dressed and studying by the time he came knocking. His pursuit of her was relentless. She was fourteen and distraught when her stepmother blamed her rather than Seymour, at least until her deathbed accusations set in motion the chain of events that would see Elizabeth cross-questioned by the council for the first time in her life as Seymour ended his life upon the scaffold. Nor had her sister Mary's marriage exactly inspired Elizabeth with much hope for future marital bliss. She had seen the uprising in Kent which was caused, however ostensibly, by the prospect of a queen marrying abroad. Elizabeth was also jealous of her power, possessive of her position, and in love with the panoply and prestige of sovereignty. Since women were expected to obey their husbands in all things, marriage to any man would dilute Elizabeth's independence and this was something she had absolutely no intention of doing. She once told a group of courtiers, 'I will have here but one mistress, and master', and she meant it.

But if she did not want a husband, might she not amuse herself by taking a lover? A whole host of candidates were suggested by gossip – Sir Christopher Hatton, John de Vere, Earl of Oxford, Sir Walter Raleigh and Robert Devereux, Earl of Essex, who was thirty-two years her junior. She was certainly in love, and visibly so, with her childhood playmate, Lord Robert Dudley, an elder brother of Jane Grey's butchered husband Guildford. Dudley had gone into the Tower under Mary I at the same time as Elizabeth, he too had lost a parent to the executioner's block and he had remained steadfastly loyal to Elizabeth throughout the difficult

Opposite: A letter from Elizabeth I. She was particularly proud of her ornate and regal signature. (Courtesy of Stephen Porter)

Elizabeth I at prayer, from the frontispiece of *Christian Prayers* (1569). She was a devout but not a fanatical Protestant. (Courtesy of Jonathan Reeve JR1168b4fp747 15501600)

Robert Dudley, Earl of Leicester, in old age.
(Courtesy of Ripon Cathedral)

years before her succession. Dudley, who was given command of the queen's horses and was thus in her company daily since Elizabeth was an active sportswoman, was also attractive, cocky and argumentative. The couple clearly adored each other and both then and later speculation ran rampant that Elizabeth had allowed Dudley into her bed. If there was anyone, it was Dudley. But Elizabeth hotly denied this, even on what she thought was her deathbed when she was struck down by smallpox in 1562, and she swore on damnation of her soul that she had never been Robert Dudley's lover. She also acidly told a nosey Spanish ambassador that it was impossible for a queen to take a lover because servants slept in her bedchamber and their dismissal would be a cause for comment: 'I do not live in a corner. A thousand eyes see all I do, and calumny will not fasten on me for ever.' Although it will never be possible to prove it one way or the other, and despite centuries of raised eyebrows and smirks about the Virgin Queen's sex life, there is in fact no evidence whatsoever to suggest that she had any lovers, and there is quite a bit to suggest she had none. She could not marry Robert Dudley even if she wanted to, because he was already married, and when his wife, Amy Robsart, was found dead at the bottom of a stairwell the ensuing scandal was so great that Elizabeth did everything in her power to strangle rumours of her own interest in Dudley, only returning royal favour to him once a coroners' inquest returned a verdict of suicide.

THE THREAT OF MARY, QUEEN OF SCOTS

Elizabeth was, like Dudley, a confirmed Protestant, but she did not seem to care much for the dogmatic disputes that were tearing her generation apart. 'There is but one Jesus Christ,' she remarked, 'all the rest is a dispute over trifles.' Early in the reign, she passed two acts, Uniformity and Settlement, which re-established the English Church's independence from Rome and created a liberal Anglican settlement which she hoped could be embraced by the majority of Catholics, whose continued support for her despite her religion was one of Elizabeth's favourite kinds of acclamation, especially when the Catholic monarchy across the Channel was busy proclaiming that as a heretic bastard she had no right to the crown, and that it should instead pass to her second cousin Mary, Queen of Scots, who was also, not coincidentally, married to the French king's eldest son.

But in 1569 the queen's certainty in the universal nature of her popularity was badly shaken by the revolt of the Northern earls, an aristocratic uprising that sought to re-establish the nobility's medieval independence from London and which also rapidly acquired a Catholic hue as part of its *cri de guerre*. The Pope, the militant and bombastic Pius V, poured fuel on the flames by excommunicating Elizabeth, denouncing her as 'the servant of crime', absolving all Catholics of obedience to a Protestant who, axiomatically in his eyes, could not be a lawful monarch, and praising any future assassination attempts against her as worthy and holy deeds. The reaction in England was vitriolic, with the excommunication of the queen tripping the wire of long-festering sectarian tensions. It also provided fodder to the growing number of hard-line Protestants who surrounded Elizabeth, including Robert Dudley, who earned himself more than one of Elizabeth's blistering, acid-tongued tirades when he tried to push her further than she was prepared to go. English and Welsh Catholics largely regarded their spiritual leader's assault on their queen with horror, realising that the far-away Pope had left them defenceless against a merciless secular authority that began to hand down fines, imprisonments and even the death sentence to anyone who still practised the old ways, all under the pretext that Catholicism now constituted a threat to Elizabeth's life. Elizabeth was not naturally bloodthirsty for Catholic lives and when she could, she attempted to ameliorate Parliament and the populace's growing savagery. During one spate of executions of fugitive Catholic priests, the local authorities confessed that they would have executed more but 'the Queen forbad it'.

This view of Catholicism as a sinister fifth column corrupting and threatening the realm from within found its spectral figurehead in the form of Elizabeth's

Scottish cousin Mary, whose first husband, King François II of France, had died prematurely, leaving his gorgeous widow to return to a country she had last seen as a child and which she barely understood or remembered. A Catholic princess raised to be charming and charmed in the luxurious chateaux of her French relatives, Mary's reign among Scotch Presbyterians burning with zeal for their cause was a disaster, culminating in the murder of her Catholic secretary, a rebellion, the traumatised queen's separation from her infant son James and her enforced flight abroad. When she arrived in northern England as a refugee from her rebellious subjects, Mary expected Elizabeth to honour the solidarity of kinship by providing her with help to ride north and crush the insurrection. Instead, Elizabeth, who was both obsessed with and distrustful of her cousin despite never meeting her, placed her under a decorous form of house arrest, providing her with a lavish allowance – an unusual piece of generosity from Elizabeth, who had inherited her grandfather Henry VII's parsimony. Elizabeth relentlessly questioned anyone who had met Mary about the Scottish queen's beauty, which was considerable, her elegance, which was even greater, and her charisma, yet greater still. She distrusted Mary's ability to charm the birds from the trees, not, when all things were considered, too dissimilar to her own, but despite this animosity and Mary's increasingly acrimonious letters bewailing her treatment, Elizabeth also defended her cousin against Protestant demands via Parliament and public opinion, which wanted the Catholic heiress apparent executed. Pressure on Elizabeth to marry and produce an heir mounted in the hope of knocking Mary out of the running, but to her advisers' frustration Elizabeth would not consider it and she confided in the Earl of Sussex that the idea had always terrified her.

The militant Catholic segments intrigued to free Mary, murder Elizabeth and place Mary, a great-granddaughter of Henry VII on her father's side, on the English and Irish thrones. When each new plot was discovered, usually thanks to the endeavours of Elizabeth's spymaster Francis Walsingham and his army of informers, Elizabeth reacted by ordering the execution of everyone involved, with the exception of Mary herself, who was always spared, to Walsingham's despair and the consternation of Elizabeth's closest adviser, Lord Burghley, who thought the queen was behaving with womanish weakness in protecting a viper in the national garden. Then, in 1586, Walsingham laid seemingly cast-iron proof that Mary had herself consented to a plot led by a group of high-ranking Catholics who would murder Elizabeth in Mary's name. Public opinion, court and Parliament were screaming for Mary's blood, the evidence against her seemed overwhelming and Elizabeth, hemmed in on all sides, signed her cousin's death warrant. When the sentence was carried out at

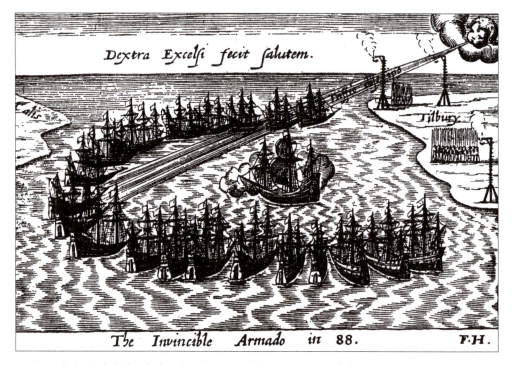

Dextra Excelsi fecit salutem.

Tilbury

Calis

The Invincible Armado in 88.

F·H·

A patriotic English sketch showing the 'invincible' Spanish Armada being scattered by the wind blowing from Heaven. (Courtesy of Jonathan Reeve JR216b5p148 15501600)

Fotheringhay Castle on 8 February 1587, Elizabeth suffered a nervous breakdown, flying around her apartments in fits of unhinged fury, sending the messenger who delivered the warrant to imprisonment in the Tower, lashing out at her advisers, writing letters to Mary's estranged son, King James VI of Scots, protesting her innocence and behaving with such genuine horror that even her closest friends could never tell whether she actually believed, as she claimed, that she was innocent of all blame. Her emotional agony certainly contrasted with the steely resignation with which her elder sister had dispatched Jane Grey, but it also showed Elizabeth as both personally and politically pathetic. For all of her consummate statecraft, she had been bounced into making a decision which, with her belief in the sacred nature of royal blood, she evidently found abhorrent.

GLORIANA

In the aftermath of Mary's execution, the Spanish Armada was launched against England after thirty years of deteriorating relations thanks to differences in religion, competition over the colonisation of the New World, Elizabeth's support for Protestant Dutch rebels against Hapsburg dominance of their homeland, and

Sir Francis Drake, one of Elizabeth's most famous captains in the fight against the Spanish. (Courtesy of Jonathan Reeve JR191b4p830 15501600)

Spanish support for the more extreme elements of the exiled English Catholic community. The Armada, scuttled by a strong wind – the blast of God's nostrils according to elated English Protestants – was Elizabeth's shining moment, the apotheosis of her career as virgin mother of her people. She appeared among the troops, encased in armour, a magnificent, fire-breathing warrior queen, summoning up the ghost of Boadicea, delivering soul-tingling speeches and proclaiming, despite her advisers' insistence that she should flee in case the Spanish succeeded, her resolve to 'live and die amongst you all; to lay down for my God, and for my kingdom, and my people, my honour and my blood, even in the dust'. But in the midst of the victory celebrations Elizabeth received the devastating news that her former beau and lifelong friend Robert Dudley, Earl of Leicester, had died while visiting a spa town. Although he had wounded her greatly by remarrying to one of her Boleyn cousins, Laetitia, and irritated her with his support for the Puritan cause, Elizabeth was grief-stricken at his passing, and his final epistle to her still survives, with the heartbreaking label 'His Last Letter' written in the queen's own handwriting.

A dying Elizabeth, hemmed in by the only two enemies she could not defeat – Father Time, on her left, and Death himself, on her right. Her last years were agonised and marred by depression. (Courtesy of Jonathan Reeve JR1719b89fpiii 16001700)

WAS ELIZABETH I BALD?

Elizabeth I nearly died after she caught smallpox in 1562 and many wondered if the fantastic wigs she wore later in her life were a result of her hair falling out during her recovery. Novels and movies made the theory famous in the twentieth century, with Bette Davis's Elizabeth pulling back her nightcap to show Joan Collins' Bess Throckmorton her bald scalp in the 1955 *The Virgin Queen*. But in 1600, when Elizabeth was in her sixties, the Earl of Essex barged into her rooms to talk to her about the Irish rebellion while Elizabeth's ladies-in-waiting were still performing her morning toilette. One irritated courtier wrote later that the earl had violated etiquette by disturbing the queen and her women when she was 'newly up, her hair about her face', which suggests she kept her natural hair well into old age. The wigs were a fashion statement, or a piece of vanity, not a cover-up.

The Puritans, the most zealous of England's Protestants, increasingly dominated and irritated Elizabeth in the final decade of her reign. She regarded many of her own co-religionists with sizzling dislike, objecting to their fundamentalist interpretation of the Bible and appalled at their insistence that it was for the people to decide if their monarch was sufficiently godly to warrant their obedience. Luckily, in an age when its approval was necessary for the granting of revenue and taxes, Elizabeth knew how to wrap Parliament around her little finger when it came to money, if not religion, and she did it by laying on the flattery and rhetoric with a trowel. Only very rarely did she lose her temper with them, once snapping when Parliament tried to dictate the monarchy's next course of action, 'It is monstrous that the feet should direct the head.' In her brighter moods, she was a superb public speaker, with a panache for hyperbolic oratory that has seldom been matched in royal history. But even her silver tongue could not spare Elizabeth from the ravages of both weather and time.

THE OLD WOMAN ON THE THRONE

The last fifteen years of Elizabeth's reign saw her physical decline, the death of many of her closest friends and advisers, a terrifyingly bloody rebellion against her in Ireland, led by the Earl of Tyrone, terrible weather, a run of resultant bad harvests which fed inflation, and the rise of a new clique of bright young things at court, impatient with the queen's suffocating conservatism and eager for change. All of her life, Elizabeth's own intellectual acumen had been supplemented by her choice of advisers, many of whom worked hard in her service and who, in contrast to her father who had condemned so many of his to the executioner's block, she remained loyal to, even if she disagreed with them, as she had with the death of Mary, Queen of Scots, in 1587. When Lord Burghley, a politician so close to her that she had nicknamed him 'my Spirit', lay dying in 1598, Elizabeth came to keep vigil at his bedside with his family, tenderly feeding him soup as he slipped in and out of consciousness.

By the turn of the century, the aging queen, increasingly a bizarre sight in layers of thick white make-up and enormous bejewelled gowns (she had nearly 3,000 by the time she died) with plunging necklines, the mark of an unmarried girl, found herself surrounded by men young enough to be her children, some of whom could not hide their contempt for the 'old woman' on the throne. The make-up was not just about vanity, it was also a mask, for it was better for Elizabeth to look strange, almost inhuman, than to appear weak and frail. When one of her young favourites, the temperamental Earl of Essex, who possessed an ego not quite commensurate to his talents, led a rebellion against her in 1601, chafing at her refusal to give him more power, he was surprised to find the city of London still loyal to her, despite the economic downturn and dissatisfaction with the government. The playwright Ben Jonson was tossed into prison for writing a scurrilous play criticising Elizabeth's rapacious advisers, but even he did not dare imply any criticism of Gloriana herself, satirical or otherwise. At least not until long after she was dead.

Elizabeth's cousin, the Countess of Nottingham, passed away in 1602, and from that point on the queen's own unravelling proved rapid. With her mind still sharp as a tack, her godson Sir John Harington was surprised to see her so despondent. She sighed a lot, she had a throat infection, swallowing became excruciating and she fought her own body trying to hide the depression and the decline. Remembering how everyone had abandoned her sister Mary I as she lay dying, Elizabeth kept her courtiers guessing about who should succeed her, although she made arch comments indicating that she did not want any offspring of the Grey sisters, one of whom had tried to steal Mary's throne, and in the process Elizabeth's, fifty years earlier. Energetic walks in the palace gardens were followed by an extraordinary stint which saw her stand, staring off into space, for fourteen solid hours without sitting down, a remarkable display of mind over matter. When one of the new bloods tried to get her into bed, to make a good death rather than a strange one, he used the mistake of using the word 'must'. Elizabeth turned to him, imperious to the last, and told him, 'Little man, the word "must" is not used to princes.' In her own time, she took to her bed and according to her godson, she sailed quietly into the night. When the Archbishop of Canterbury came to keep vigil, she shook her head when he tried to pray for her longer life, but when he began to talk quietly to her of the joys of Salvation and Christ's promise of Heaven, Elizabeth 'hugged his hand' according to eyewitnesses. Then, 'like a lamb', she closed her eyes on 24 March 1603 and a distant Boleyn relative took a ring from her hand to ride north to proclaim a new king, a new dynasty, in the person of King James VI of Scots, Henry VII's great-great-grandson and the only child of Mary, Queen of Scots. A clever man, who came south with Anna, his manipulative and glamorous Danish queen, and their tribe of children, James was the first king of the Stuart dynasty to unite the thrones of England, Ireland and Scotland. His reign was to prove troubled and his son's more so; their difficulties have led to some historians suspecting that Elizabeth's reputation for greatness, as Elizabeth Gloriana, was a later invention, caused by comparing her to the problems faced and caused by the Stuarts. However, she was a brilliant monarch – loyal to well-chosen advisers, intellectually accomplished and charming. She was a woman who had devoted herself to preserving stability in all its forms, and, in doing so, allowed her kingdoms to enjoy half a century of relative peace, which allowed the flourishing of the arts and architecture for which her reign is so justly famous. For centuries, people have been trying to make sense of her, and the recent bizarre theories that she must have suffered from testicular feminisation, that she was essentially hermaphroditic, or in some way anything other than a biological woman, shows that we are still incapable of accepting a biologically normal woman as a powerful figure. All the conspiracy theories about Elizabeth I's aberrant sex life, confused gender, and physical abnormalities tell us much about ourselves and almost nothing about her.

At Elizabeth's death, some, knowing of the recent economic troubles and the sympathy for those who had criticised her, thought the people would remain indifferent to Elizabeth's passing, but the crowds wept as her body was borne through the streets of London towards Westminster Abbey to rest with her ancestors.

WHAT NEXT?

Non-Fiction

Baldwin Smith, Lacey, *A Tudor Tragedy: The Life and Times of Catherine Howard* (New York, 1963)

Bordo, Susan, *The Creation of Anne Boleyn: In Search of the Tudors' Most Notorious Queen* (New York, 2013)

Brigden, Susan, *New Worlds, Lost Worlds: The Rule of the Tudors, 1485–1603* (London, 2000)

De Lisle, Leanda, *The Sisters Who Would be Queen: The Tragedy of Mary, Katherine and Lady Jane Grey* (London, 2008).

De Lisle, Leanda, *Tudor: The Family Story* (London, 2013)

Fraser, Antonia, *The Six Wives of Henry VIII* (London, 1992)

Guy, John, *Tudor England* (Oxford University Press, 1990)

Ives, Eric, *The Life and Death of Anne Boleyn: The Most Happy* (Oxford, 2004)

Matusiak, John, *Henry VIII: The Life and Rule of England's Nero* (Stroud, 2013)

Norton, Elizabeth, *Catherine Parr* (Stroud, 2011)

Penn, Thomas, *Winter King: The Dawn of Tudor England* (London, 2012)

Porter, Linda, *Mary Tudor: The First Queen* (London 2007)

Ridgway, Claire, *The Fall of Anne Boleyn: A Countdown* (Lúcar, 2012)

Skidmore, Chris, *Edward VI: The Lost King of England* (London, 2008)

Somerset, Anne, *Elizabeth I* (London, 2002)

Starkey, David, *Elizabeth: Apprenticeship* (London, 2000)

Starkey, David, *Six Wives: The Queens of Henry VIII* (London, 2003)

Tremlett, Giles, *Catherine of Aragon: Henry's Spanish Queen* (London, 2010)

Weir, Alison, *The Lady in the Tower: The Fall of Anne Boleyn* (London, 2009)

Whitelock, Anna, *Mary Tudor: England's First Queen* (London, 2010)

Wilson, A. N., *The Elizabethans* (London, 2012)

Wilson, Derek, *A Brief History of Henry VIII: Reformer and Tyrant* (London, 2009)

Fiction

George, Margaret, *Autobiography of Henry VIII* (Pan, 2012)

Mantel, Hilary, *Wolf Hall* (Fourth Estate, 2010)

Sansom, C. J., *Sovereign* (Pan, 2007)

TV and Film

A Man for All Seasons (1966)

Anne of the Thousand Days (1969)

Elizabeth R (BBC, 1971)

INDEX

Also in the Illustrated Introductions series

Fascinated by history? Wish you knew more?
The Illustrated Introductions are here to help.

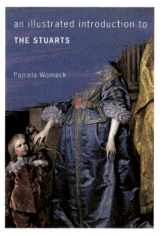

An Illustrated Introduction to the
Stuarts

978-1-4456-3788-4
£9.99

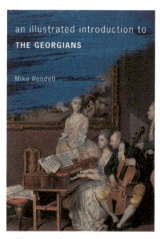

An Illustrated Introduction to the
Georgians

978-1-4456-3630-6
£9.99
Available from November 2014

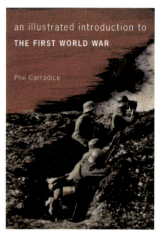

An Illustrated Introduction to the
First World War

978-1-4456-3296-4
£9.99

An Illustrated Introduction to the
Second World War

978-1-4456-3848-5
£9.99